The Cabinet Gallery and Compendium of Shakespeare's Dramatic Works

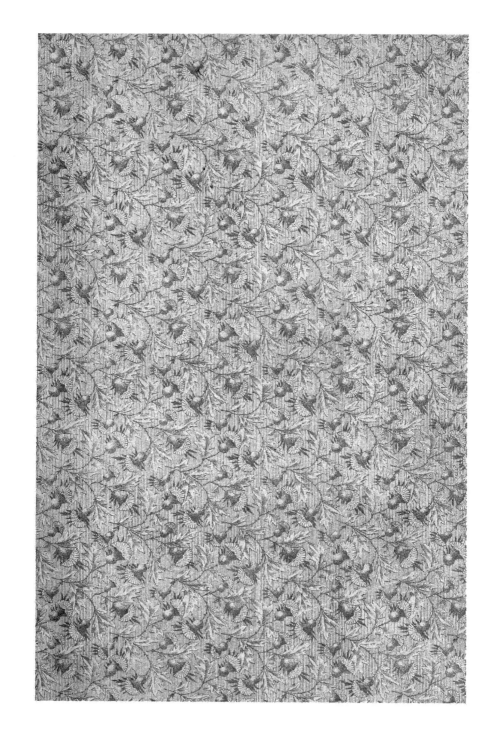

THE

CABINET GALLERY

AND COMPENDIUM

OF

SHAKESPEARE'S DRAMATIC WORKS

WILLIAM SHAKESPEARE.
(Chandos Portrait)

THE

CABINET GALLERY

AND COMPENDIUM

OF

SHAKESPEARE'S DRAMATIC WORKS

EACH DRAMA ILLUSTRATED AND BRIEFLY
OUTLINED

EDITED BY
GEO. A. SMITH, B. A.

FIFTY-ONE PHOTOGRAVURES ON STEEL

PHILADELPHIA
GEBBIE & CO., PUBLISHERS
1890

PREFACE

IT is the aim of the publishers to make this COM-
PENDIUM such a perfect summary of Shakespeare's
Dramas as will enable the student to comprehend the
whole plot of each play at a glance. This will be
found a great advantage to the general reader, and will
prove a still greater boon to the theatre-goer who may
be about to witness on the stage one of Shakespeare's
plays which he may not have read, or read so long ago
as to need refreshing his memory thereon Each
drama will be treated separately. The following will
be the method of treatment of each drama .

1st A historical notice of when the play was
written, first printed, or first acted, and the sources
from whence Shakespeare most probably drew his
work.

2d The plot of the play summarized and the
dramatis personœ in this connection repeated in detail

3d. A few brief notes on the most prominent
characters in each drama, to enable the reader more

readily to measure and estimate the relative importance and position of the chief actors engaged

This arrangement for busy men and women will possess at least the recommendation of novelty, and we think will be found generally useful, when any play of Shakespeare is spoken of, to be able at a few minutes' notice to compass an understanding of all the chief characters and the plot of the drama.

A separate INDEX OF CHARACTERS will be found following the Compendium We believe this is the first time that all the characters in Shakespeare's works have been brought together and registered each in their proper place.

GEBBIE & Co.

CONTENTS.

(1)

2   CONTENTS.

PHOTOGRAVURE ILLUSTRATIONS.

3

W. VON KAULBACH, PINX.

CALIBAN, STEPHANO AND TRINCULO.

The Tempest. Act II. Scene II.

HISTORICAL SUMMARY OF THE TEMPEST

No one has hitherto been foi tunate enough to discover the romance, on which Shakespeare founded this play. Mr Collins, the poet, issaid indeed to have infoimed Mr. T Warton, that it was founded on an old romance called 'Auielio and Isabella,' printed in Italian, Spanish, French and English in 1588; but as no such work could be discovered by the acute and learned writer to whom this information was communicated, it was reasonably inferred by him, that Collins, in consequence of the failure of memory during his last illness, had substituted the name of one novel for another

It seems probable, that the event, which immediately gave rise to the composition of this drama, was the voyage of Sir George Someis, who was shipwrecked on the Bermudas in 1609, and whose adventures were given to the public by Silvester Jourdan, one of his crew, with the following title 'A Discovery of the Bermudas, otherwise called the Isle of Divels · by Sir Thomas Gates, Sir Geoige Someis, and Captayne Newport, and divers others.' In this publication Jouidan informs us, that 'the islands of the Bermudas, as every man knoweth, that hath heard or read of them, were never inhabited by any Christian or heathen people , but ever esteemed and reputed a most prodigious and enchanted place, affoiding nothing but gusts, stormes and foul weather; which made every navigator and mariner to avoid them as Scylla and Charybdis, or as they would shun the devil himselfe ' It has hence been concluded that this play was written towards the close of 1611, and that it was brought on the stage early in the succeeding year

Mr Hunter says, there is an island in the Mediterranean named Lampedosa, which is near to the coast of Tunis, and from its description in Dapper, was the probable track of the King of Naples' voyage in Shakespeare's 'Tempest' This island is known to sailors as the enchanted island, and if the Italian novel or its translations should ever be discovered, it will be found that this surmise is correct

It is remarked by Dr Drake, that 'the 'Tempest' is, next to Macbeth, the noblest product of our author's genius Never were the wild and the wonderful, the pathetic and the sublime, more artfully and gracefully combined with the sportive sallies of a playful imagination, than in this enchantingly attractive drama Nor is it less remarkable, that all these excellences of the highest order are connected with a plot, which, in its mechanism, and in the preservation of the unities, is perfectly classical and correct '

PERSONS REPRESENTED.

ALONSO, king of Naples
SEBASTIAN, his brother
PROSPERO, the rightful duke of Milan.
ANTONIO, his brother, the usurping duke of Milan.
FERDINAND, son to the king of Naples.

GONZALO, an honest old counsellor of Naples.

ADRIAN, } lords.
FRANCISCO,

CALIBAN, a savage and deformed slave, found by Prospero on the desert island.

TRINCULO, a jester
STEPHANO, a drunken butler
MASTER of a ship, BOATSWAIN, and MARINERS.

MIRANDA, daughter to Prospero.
ARIEL, an airy spirit

IRIS,
CERES,
JUNO, } spirits.
NYMPHS,
REAPERS,

Other spirits attending on Prospero.

SCENE, the sea, with a ship; afterwards an uninhabited island

---

COMPENDIUM OF THE PLAY

PROSPERO, duke of Milan, being fond of study and retirement, intrusts the public business of the state to his younger brother Antonio, who secretly engages with Alonso, king of Naples, to hold Milan as a fief of the Neapolitan crown, in consideration of his assistance in dethroning his unsuspecting brother. Not daring publicly to deprive Prospero of life, on account of his great popularity, the conspirators force him and his daughter Miranda, an infant three years

old, into a crazy boat; and with a small supply of
provisions abandon them to the fury of the elements Being cast on a desert island, wheie no
human creature is found but a savage named Caliban, Prospero puts into practice the neciomantic art,
with which he had formerly experimented, with
great success, and employed his leisure hours with
the education of Miranda About twelve years after
these transactions, Alonso, having agreed to many
his daughter to the king of Tunis, conducts her to
that country, accompanied by the usurping duke of
Milan, and a numerous train. Having left the
lady with her husband at Tunis, they embark on
their return to Naples, and the drama commences
with a great tempest raised by Prospeio, who, by
the agency of a spirit named Aiiel, wrecks the
king's ship in such a manner, that none of the passengers are lost, and they are all landed on Prospero's
island Ferdinand, the king's son, is sepaiated fiom
his father, who supposes him drowned, while Pios-
pero, discovering him after the shipwreck, conducts
him to his cell, where he and Miranda become
mutually enamored. In the mean time, Alonso,
Antonio and their immediate followers, terrified by
spectral illusions raised by the injured duke, iun
distracted, till at length, Prospero, satisfied with making them sensible of their former guilt, and with the
resumption of his dignity, generously remits further
punishment, extends his mercy to Caliban and his
drunken companions, who had conspired to muider
him; and, having restoied Ferdinand to his disconsolate parent, abjures forever the magic art, and
proceeds to Naples to solemnize the nuptials of the
youthful pair. Like the 'Midsummer Night's

W. VON KAULBACH, PINX.

FERDINAND AND MIRANDA.

The Tempest, Act IV, Scene I.

Dream,' with which it has been classed, the 'Tempest.' is one of those romantic dramas, which defy analytical criticism, and would lose in effect by being subjected to a rigid examination of realities. Although the unities are preserved, perhaps more by accident than design, no play owes less allegiance to the exact sciences, and the interest is not weakened by trivial incongruities in the author's conduct of time and space. A hag-born monster, a young lady educated by a magician prince in a desolate island, and an attendant spirit, capable of the assumption of any form, who not only treads the ooze of the salt deep, runs on the sharp wind of the north, works in the frosted earth, and rides on the curled clouds, but in his lighter moods, rides on the bat's back, or reposes in a cowslip's bell, are singular materials for a drama, the simplicity of whose construction exhibits in strong outline the boundless skill by which it is made so irresistibly attractive It required the genius of Shakespeare to reconcile these apparently discordant elements, and construct out of them an harmonious structure. If, however, the reader imagines a defect exists, and agreeing with some critics in the opinion that Ariel was not an 'ethereal featureless angel,' observes an inconsistency in the development of his character, let us entreat him to merge it into the romantic conduct of the plot, and regard the whole drama as a purely imaginative construction formed on the idea of retributive justice, to which no one but Shakespeare has made necromancy subservient, without in some degree injuring the cause of virtue.

HISTORICAL SUMMARY OF THE TWO GEN-
TLEMEN OF VERONA.

MR STEEVENS conjectures that some of the incidents of this play were taken by Shakespeare from the 'Arcadia,' book 1 chap. 6, where Pyrocles consents to head the Helots , to which tale the adventures of Valentine with the outlaws, in this drama, bear a striking resemblance   But however this question may be disposed of there can be little doubt that the episode of Felismena, in the Diana of George of Montemayor, a romance translated from the Spanish, and published in the year 1598, was the source whence the principal part of the plot of the 'Two Gentlemen of Verona' has been derived   The story of Proteus and Julia, in this play, closely corresponds with its prototype , and in several passages the dramatist has copied the very language of the pastoral

The authenticity of this drama has been disputed by Hanmer, Theobald, and Upton, who condemn it as a very inferior production · but Dr Johnson, in ascribing it to the pen of Shakespeare, asks, 'if it be taken from him, to whom shall it be given ? ' justly remarking, that ' it will be found more creditable that Shakespeare might sometimes sink below his highest flights, than that any other should rise up to his lowest.' ' It is observable,' says Pope, ' that the style of this comedy is less figurative, and more natural and unaffected, than the greater part of this author's, though supposed to be one of the first he wrote.'

FROM A DAGUERROTYPE BY PAINE.

MR. COMPTON AS LAUNCE.

Two Gentlemen of Verona. Act IV. Scene IV.

The 'Two Gentlemen of Verona' was,not printed until it appeared in the folio of 1623, but is mentioned in Meres' 'Wits' Treasury,' printed in 1598.

PERSONS REPRESENTED.

DUKE of Milan, father to Silvia.

VALENTINE, } gentlemen of Verona
PROTEUS,

ANTONIO, father to Proteus

THURIO, a foolish rival to Valentine.

EGLAMOUR, agent for Silvia in her escape.

SPEED, a clownish servant to Valentine

LAUNCE, servant to Proteus

PANTHINO, servant to Antonio.

HOST, where Julia lodges in Milan

OUTLAWS.

JULIA, a lady of Verona, beloved by Proteus.

SILVIA, the duke's daughter, beloved by Valentine.

LUCETTA, waiting-woman to Julia.

Servants, Musicians

SCENE, sometimes in Verona; sometimes in Milan; and on the frontiers of Mantua

COMPENDIUM OF THE PLAY.

A young gentleman of Verona, named Valentine, after taking leave of his friend Proteus, visits the court

of Milan, where he becomes captivated by the
charms of Silvia, the duke's daughter, who secretly
favors his addresses, in preference to those of a rich
suitor provided by her father. In the mean time,
Proteus, who had become enamored of Julia, a
Veronese lady, successfully prosecutes his suit, and
obtains from his mistress assurances of mutual regard. The satisfaction of these lovers is soon interrupted by the young gentleman's father, who, ignorant of his son's attachment, is anxious to send him
to Milan, where Valentine still resides After quitting Julia with professions of unalterable constancy,
Proteus joins his friend, who receives him with the
utmost tenderness; confides to him the secret of his
love, and, having introduced him into the presence
of Silvia, informs him of his intended elopement
with her but he has soon reason to repent his
misplaced confidence, for Proteus, a very inferior
character, who by this time had forgotten his
vows to Julia, and was resolved to supplant Valentine, treacherously informs the duke of his daughter's proposed flight, which procures the banishment
of Valentine and the imprisonment of Silvia
During this period, Julia, unable to endure the
absence of her lover, travels to Milan in the disguise of a youth, and contrives to hire herself as a
page to Proteus, whose perfidy she soon discovers
Silvia soon after effects her escape from confinement,
but is overtaken in a forest by Proteus, who endeavors to obtain her consent by threats of violence,
when she is unexpectedly rescued by Valentine,
whose life had recently been spared by a band of
outlaws settled here, on condition of becoming their
leader. The remonstrances of Valentine awaken

the remorse of Proteus   he entreats forgiveness,
which is readily granted him ; and Julia, having
discovered herself, is united to her lover ; while the
duke, after pardoning the outlaws and recalling
them from exile, willingly consents to the nuptials
of his daughter with Valentine   Speed and Launce,
servants respectively to Valentine and Proteus, are
droll fellows—Launce with his dog in the fourth act
is a masterpiece of wit and funny invention   Mr
Halliwell says, "Although probably not quite the
'first heir' of Shakespeare's dramatic invention, the
'Two Gentlemen of Verona' exhibits a deficiency of
effective situation, and to some extent a crudity of
construction, which would most likely have been
avoided by a practised writer for the stage   But
these defects are unnoticed by the reader in the
richness of its poetical beauties and overflowing
humor , its romance and pathos   The tale is based
on love and friendship   Valentine is the ideal personification of both, of pure love to Silvia, and
romantic attachment to the friend of his youth
Proteus, on the contrary, selfish and sensual, suffers
himself to be guided by his passions, and concludes
his inconstancy to his love with perfidious treachery
to his friend   Valentine, noble and brave, but timid
before the mistress of his affections, adoring Silvia's
glove, and too diffident even to interpret her stratagem of the letter · Proteus, daring all, and losing
his integrity. in the excess of a tumultuous passion
If Shakespeare has painted these elements in an outline something too bold for the extreme refinement
of the present day, the error must be ascribed to his
era, not to himself, and if it be also objected to in
this play, that the female characters are germs only

of more powerful creations in 'Twelfth Night' or 'Cymbeline,' the reader must bear in mind they are perhaps more suitable to the extreme simplicity of the story, that the chief object of the dramatist is directed to the development of the characters of Valentine and Proteus, and, above all, that the play should be judged by itself.   There are few, indeed, who would be willing to miss the 'Two Gentlemen of Verona,' for it is, nevertheless, a gem, though it may not shine quite as brilliantly as some others in the Shakesperian cabinet."

FROM A PHOTOGRAPH BY SARONY.

ADA REHAN AND MISS DREHER AS MRS. FORD AND MRS. PAGE.

Merry Wives of Windsor, Act II. Scene I.

HISTORICAL SUMMARY OF THE MERRY WIVES OF WINDSOR.

An old translation of 'Il Pecorone,' by Giovanni Florentino, is supposed to have furnished Shakespeare with some of the incidents of this comedy.

Mr Rowe informs us that Queen Elizabeth was so well pleased with the admirable character of Falstaff in the two parts of Henry IV that she commanded our author to continue it for one play more, and to show him in love; a task which he is said to have completed in a fortnight, to the admiration of his royal patroness, who was afterwards very well pleased at the representation   This information, it is probable, came originally from Dryden, who, from his intimacy with Sir William Davenant, had an opportunity of learning many particulars concerning Shakespeare   Mr Chalmers has endeavored to set aside the general tradition relative to this comedy, but does not appear to have succeeded

Speaking of this play, Dr Johnson remarks that 'no task is harder than that of writing to the ideas of another. Shakespeare knew what the queen, if the story be true, seems not to have known ,—that by any real passion of tenderness, the selfish craft, the careless jollity, and the lazy luxury of Falstaff must have suffered so much abatement that little of his former cast would have remained   Falstaff could not love but by ceasing to be Falstaff   He could only counter-
16

feit love, and his professions could be prompted, not by the love of pleasure, but of money. Thus the poet approached as neaɪ as he could to the work enjoined him : yet having, perhaps, ɪn hɪs former plays completed hɪs own idea, seems not to have been able to give Falstaff all hɪs former power of entertainment

This comedy was not prɪnted in ɪts present form tɪll 1623, when ɪt was published with the rest of Shakespeare's plays ɪn the folɪo edɪtɪon   An imperfect copy had been prɪnted in 1602

PERSONS REPRESENTED.

Sir JOHN FALSTAFF
FENTON, a young gentleman in love with Anne Page.
SHALLOW, a country ᴊustɪce.
SLENDER, cousin to Shallow.
Mr FORD, } two gentlemen dwelling at Wɪndsor.
Mr PAGE, }
WILLIAM PAGE, a boy, ŝon to Mr. Page.
Sɪr HUGH EVANS, a Welsh parson.
Dr CAIUS, a French physician.
HOST of the Garter Inn
BARDOLPH, }
PISTOL,   } followers of Falstaff.
NYM,   }
ROBIN, page to Falstaff
SIMPLE, servant to Slender
RUGBY, servant to Dr Caius

Mrs FORD, } the merry wives.
Mrs PAGE, }

E.GRÜTZNER,PINX.

FALSTAFF AND MRS. FORD.

Merry Wives of Windsor, Act III, Scene III.

Mrs ANNE PAGE, her daughter, in love with Fenton.
Mrs QUICKLY, servant to Dr Caius

Servants to Page, Ford, etc.

SCENE, Windsor, and the parts adjacent.

COMPENDIUM OF THE PLAY.

THE vanity of Sir John Falstaff having misinterpreted
the hospitable attentions of two ladies (The Merry
Wives) at Windsor into an admiration for his person, he resolves to profit by his good fortune, but is
betrayed by some discarded domestics (Pistol and
Bardolph) who revenge their dismissal by revealing
their master's designs to the husbands of his mistresses.   Page disregards the information altogether;
while Ford, who had, for some time past, entertained
unfounded suspicions of his wife's honor, resolves
to ascertain the truth of the information.   For this
purpose, under the assumed name of Brook, he
causes himself to be introduced to Falstaff, whom
he artfully draws into the confession of an assignation which he had just before made with mistress
Ford, who in the meantime had conspired with her
friend to punish the knight for his infamous propo-
sals   Ford, supposing that he has sufficiently de-
tected the infidelity of his wife, assembles his neighbors, in order to surprise Falstaff at the appointed
interview . he is, however, conveyed away, by the
contrivance of the two wives, in a basket with foul

linen, and thrown into the Thames, where he narrowly escapes drowning. The suspicions of Ford are now somewhat abated, but when he again repairs to Falstaff as Brook, and learns the deception that has been practised on him, and the arrangements which have been made by his wife for a second visit from her admirer, his fury rekindles, he again solicits his friends to accompany him home, whence Falstaff again escapes in the disguise of an old witch, though not without suffering a severe cudgelling at the hands of the enraged Ford as a fortune-teller. A third assignation is now made with him in Windsor forest at midnight, where Falstaff, representing the spirit of Herne the huntsman, with horns on his head, having agreed to assume this disguise for a meeting with Mrs Ford and Mrs Page, is severely pinched by the accomplices of the plot, in the garb of fairies and hobgoblins; when the husbands, who are now made acquainted with the intention of their wives, rush from the place of their concealment; and, having sufficiently exposed and derided him, forgive him The remainder of this comedy is occupied by the rivalry of Slender and Caius, for the hand of Page's daughter Anne, who prefers a young gentleman named Fenton, whom she marries. Mr Singer says, "the bustle and variety of the incidents, the rich assemblage of characters, and the skilful conduct of the plot of this delightful comedy, are unrivalled in any drama, ancient or modern Falstaff, the inimitable Falstaff, here 'lards the lean earth,' a butt and a wit, a humorist, and a man of humor, a touchstone and a laughing-stock, a jester and a jest—the most perfect comic character that ever was exhibited.' The jealous Ford, the uxorious Page, and their two merry wives are admirably drawn , Sir Hugh Evans and Dr. Caius no less so, and the duel scene between them irresistibly comic   The swaggering jolly Boniface, mine host of the Garter ; and last, though not least, Master Slender and his cousin Shallow, are such a group as were never yet equalled by the pen or pencil of genius.'

HISTORICAL SUMMARY OF 'TWELFTH NIGHT.'

THE comic scenes of this play appear to have been entirely the production of our author ; while the serious part is founded on a story in the fourth volume of 'Belleforest's Histoires Tragiques,' which he took from Bandello. Malone, however, is of opinion that the plot of this comedy was rather derived from the 'Historie of Apolonius and Silla,' which tale is to be found in a collection, by Barnaby Rich, which first appeared in the year 1583 But little doubt can remain of the identity of the story of Bandello with the incidents of 'Twelfth Night,' after a perusal of the comparison of both compositions from the pen of Mrs Lennox.—

'Sebastian and Viola, in the play, are the same with Paolo and Nicuola in the novel . both are twins, and both remarkably like each other Viola is parted from her brother by a shipwreck, and supposes him to be drowned ; Nicuola loses her brother at the sacking of Rome, and for a long time is ignorant whether he is alive or dead Viola serves the duke, with whom she is in love, in the habit of a page , Nicuola, in the same disguise, attends Lattantio, who had forsaken her for Catella The duke sends Viola to solicit his mistress in his favor ; Lattantio commissions Nicuola to plead for him with Catella. The duke's mistress falls in

ELLEN TERRY AS VIOLA.

Twelfth Night. Act II, Scene II.

love with Viola, supposing her to be a man ; and
Catella, by the like mistake, is enamored of Nicuola :
and, lastly, the two ladies in the play, as well as in the
novel, marry their lovers whom they had waited on in
disguise, and their brothe s wed the ladies who had
been enamored of them '

Mr Collier and Mr Hunter almost simultaneously
discovered, in a manuscript diary of a student of the
Middle Temple, among the Harleian Manuscripts,
dating from 1601 to 1603, the following passage,
which shows that all previous speculations, with regard
to the date of the composition of this play, had
assigned it to too late a period —

"Feb 2, 1601 [2]

" At our feast, wee had a play called Twelve Night,
or What You Will   Much like the Comedy of Errors,
or Menechuri in Plautus , but most like and neere to
that in Italian called Ingauni.   A good practice in it
to make the steward believe his lady widowe was in
love with him, by counterfayting a letter as from his
lady in general terms, telling him what she liked best
in him, and prescribing his gesture in smiling, his
apparraile, etc , and then when he came to practice
making him believe they took him to be mad," etc.

Mr Hunter by unwearied investigation, and an ingenious inductive process, ascertained that the writing
of the diary was that of John Manningham, who was
entered of the Middle Temple in 1597

The play had most probably been publicly acted
before this private performance, at the Candlemas
feast of the Middle Temple in 1601-2 , and from the
absence of it in the list of Shakespeare's plays enumer-

ated by Meres in 1598, the inference is that it was composed in 1599 or 1600.

PERSONS REPRESENTED.

ORSINO, duke of Illyria, in love with Olivia
SEBASTIAN, a young gentleman, brother to Viola
ANTONIO, a sea captain, friend to Sebastian.
A SEA CAPTAIN, friend to Viola.
VALENTINE, } gentlemen attending on the duke.
CURIO,
SIR TOBY BELCH, uncle of Olivia
SIR ANDREW AGUE-CHEEK, boon companion of Sir
  Toby.
MALVOLIO, steward to Olivia.
FABIAN, } servants to Olivia.
CLOWN,

OLIVIA, a rich countess
VIOLA, in love with the duke.
MARIA, Olivia's woman

Lords, Priests, Sailors, Officers, Musicians, and other
Attendants.

SCENE, a city in Illyria and the sea-coast near it.

COMPENDIUM OF THE PLAY.

SEBASTIAN and Viola, twin children of a gentleman

E.GRUTZNER.PINX.

MALVOLIO. SIR TOBY BELCH. ETC.

Twelfth Night. Act II. Scene III.

of Messaline, and remarkable for an exact resemblance of features, being deprived of both their parents, quit their native country : they are encountered at sea by a violent tempest, which destroys the vessel and most of the crew, while Viola, the captain, and a few passengers betake themselves to the boat, which conveys them in safety to the seacoast of Illyria. The lady, thus deprived of her brother, clothes herself in male attire, and enters into the service of Prince Orsino, who is at this time engaged in the unsuccessful pursuit of a neighboring lady, named Olivia. The talents of the disguised page soon render her so great a favorite of her master, that she is selected to intercede with the obdurate Olivia ; who, though deaf to the solicitations of the prince, is seized with a sudden passion for the messenger, which meets with a repulse. Viola, on her return home, is waylaid by Sir Andrew Ague-cheek, a foolish suitor of Olivia, favored by her uncle, Sir Toby Belch, who persuades him to challenge the youth, in order to beget in his mistress a favorable opinion of his courage. Viola, as may well be supposed, is averse to a rencontre of this description ; when she is rescued from her embarrassment by the arrival of a sea captain, who, having saved her brother Sebastian from the wreck, had since supplied him with considerable sums of money for his exigencies ; but, in consequence of an unexpected arrest, is compelled to solicit a moiety of the loan : he accordingly applies to Viola, believing that he is addressing his friend Sebastian ; and, when she denies all knowledge of his person, reproaches her with her ingratitude. In the meantime, Sebastian arrives ; and the foolish knight, with his confederate, supposing him to be the page of Orsino, who had before declined the combat, assault him , but their violence is repaid with interest, and the combatants are parted by Olivia, whose advances to the supposed page are now received with mutual affection, and they are married without delay. Viola, arriving soon after with her master at the house of Olivia, is mistaken by the lady for her husband, by whose appearance the mystery is at length cleared up, and Viola is united to the prince The bye-play of the pranks of Maria, the waiting-maid of Viola, and Sir Toby Belch with Malvolio, the major-domo of Viola's household, is one of the brightest bits of fun in Shakespeare's works In the character of Malvolio some of the best Shakespearian actors have appeared, among others Charles Barron and Henry Irving What is the subject of the comedy ? Love : the Duke's love for Olivia—the love of Viola for the Duke—the new-born love of Olivia for the disguised Viola , and there is a sly penchant growing between Sir Toby and Maria—they are assimilated together by their love of fun ; and Malvolio's ridiculous love for his mistress Olivia The artist is not seen endeavoring to force a catastrophe · the characters fall into their places with a natural ease and grace, as if they were our veritable neighbors, and we already knew all about them. A noble-natured lady, mourning for her brother's death, will not for grief listen to the manly and ardent wooing of the Duke, and Viola, 'beautiful exceedingly,' whose heart has become a shrine, where in turn love for the Duke burns with a calm, undecaying constancy, yet having little or no hope of return, so that when we hear her urging Orsino's suit into Olivia's unwilling ears, we

sympathize the more strongly with her, knowing
that all ·this time runs a trembling through her
voice, which speaks more of suffering than could
many complaining words.   There is a magic in it,
too, for all that; and even the cold Olivia feels it as
the tones fall around her heart, and she, that could
not, or would not love, for very excess of grief, now
loves in despite of it, as 'twere against her will , and
we see that she had not forgotten her woman's wit
and tact, when she sends Malvolio after the ' peevish
messenger' with her ring   Illyria is a warm and
sunny clime, peculiarly so at the bright ' season of
the year,' when love most rejoices, and smiles in
the bright and beauteous face of nature with a
serener joy   The comedy is rich, hearty, rollicking,
abandoned , actually glorious in its wild, mad
revelry.

HISTORICAL SUMMARY OF 'MEASURE FOR MEASURE.'

THE primary source of the fable of this play is to
be traced to a story in the Ecatommithi of Giraldi
Cinthio, which was repeated in the tragic histories of
Belleforest, but Shakespeare's immediate original was
the play of 'Promos and Cassandra' of George Whetstone, published in 1578   'This story,' says Mr.
Steevens, 'which, in the hands of Whetstone, produced little more than barren insipidity, under the
culture of Shakespeare, became fertile of entertainment   The old play of 'Promos and Cassandra' exhibits an almost complete embryo of 'Measure for Measure,' yet the hints on which it is formed are so slight,
that it is nearly as impossible to detect them as it is to
point out in the acorn the future ramifications of the
oak '

Dr. Johnson, speaking of this play, says, 'I cannot
but suspect that some other had new-modelled the
novel of Cinthio, or written a story, which in some
particulars resembled it, and that Cinthio was not the
author whom Shakespeare immediately followed   The
emperor in Cinthio is named Maximine : the duke, in
Shakespeare's enumeration of the persons of the
drama, is called Vincentio   This appears a very slight
remark, but since the duke has no name in the play,
nor is ever mentioned but by his title, why should he
be called Vincentio among the persons but because the

A. SPIESS. PINX.

ANGELO AND ISABELLA.

Measure for Measure. Act II. Scene IV.

name was copied from the story, and placed super-
fluously at the head of the list by the mere habit of
transcription? It is therefore likely that there was
then a story of Vincentio, duke of Vienna, different
from that of Maximine, emperor of the Romans.

' Of this play, the light or comic part is very natural
and pleasing, but the grave scenes, if a few passages
be excepted, have more labor than elegance. The plot
is rather intricate than artful '

Malone concludes that ' Measure for Measure ' was
written in 1603–1604 In the latter year it was first
performed by ' His Majesty's Players ' at Whitehall.
It was first printed in the folio edition of 1623.

PERSONS REPRESENTED.

VINCENTIO, duke of Vienna.
ANGELO, lord deputy in the duke's absence
ESCALUS, an ancient lord, joined with Angelo in the
    deputation
CLAUDIO, a young gentleman
LUCIO, a fantastic
Two other like GENTLEMEN.
VARRIUS,* a gentleman, servant to the duke.
PROVOST.
THOMAS, }
PETER,   } two friars.
A JUSTICE.

* Varrius might be omitted, for he is only once spoken to,
and says nothing in reply.

ELBOW, a simple constable.
FROTH, a foolish gentleman
CLOWN, servant to Mrs Over-done.
ABHORSON, an executioner
BARNARDINE, a dissolute prisoner

ISABELLA, sister to Claudio
MARIANA, betrothed to Angelo.
JULIET, beloved by Claudio
FRANCISCA, a nun, with whom Isabella is as a novitiate
Mrs. OVER-DONE, a bawd

Lords, Gentlemen, Guards, Officers, and other
Attendants

SCENE, Vienna

COMPENDIUM OF THE PLAY.

VINCENTIO, duke of Vienna, anxious to reform the laxity of public morals, which too great remissness on the part of his government had introduced, invests Angelo, an officer renowned for rigid justice, with unlimited authority during his pretended absence , and, having assumed the habit of a friar, is enabled in this disguise to view attentively the proceedings of his deputy. A young lady of the city, named Juliet, proves pregnant by her betrothed lover, Claudio, who, according to an old penal enactment, is sentenced by the severe governor to lose his head Isabella, the sister of the culprit, inter-

cedes for the life of her brother with Angelo, who
becomes deeply enamored with her, and proposes
her dishonor as the price of his compliance with her
petition. The virtuous maiden spurns the prof-
fered terms, and flies to Claudio, to whom she relates the perfidy of the governor, exhorting him to
submit to his fate with fortitude ; but the fear of
death overpowers his resolution, and he implores his
sister to yield to the solicitations of the deputy,
which request she rejects with abhorrence. In the
meantime the disguised duke has become acquainted
with Mariana, a lady formerly affianced to Angelo,
who is persuaded to keep a private assignation with
her husband (Angelo), which Isabella has feigned to
make in her own name, to secure the safety of her
brother. The inhuman tyrant, supposing that he
has now achieved his object, and dreading the
vengeance of the injured Claudio, determines to disregard his promise of mercy, and sends orders to
the prison for his immediate execution. The duke
now pretends to return from his travels, and Angelo
is publicly convicted of murder and seduction both
by Isabella and his master ; and is about to suffer
the punishment of his crimes, when the entreaties
of his deserted wife, and the unexpected appearance of Claudio, who had been rescued from death
by the interposition of the disguised duke, preserves
him from the fate which he has so justly merited.
As a relief to the more serious business of the play
there are amusing scenes in which Froth, Elbow, a
clown, and others perform delightful low comedy.
Mr. Halliwell says : 'I think it will be found a
serious error has been committed by nearly all who
have treated on the play, in estimating the extent

of the crime for which Claudio was condemned
Ulrici says he had 'seduced his mistress befoie
marriage ' This is, however, erroneous In Shakespeare's time the ceremony of betrothment was
usually supposed to confer the power of matiimonial
union   Claudio obtained possession of Juhetta on
'a true contract ,' and provided marriage was celebrated within a reasonable time afterwards, no
criminality could be alleged after the contract had
been formally made   So, likewise, the duke tells
Mariana it was no sin to meet Angelo, for he was
her 'husband on a pre-contract '   The story would
be more pioperly analyzed by representing Claudio's
error as venial and Angelo's strictness so much the
more severe, thus involving a greater antithesis in
his fall   The only painful scene in the play is the
subject of the argument between Angelo and Isabella , but Shakespeare is not to be blamed for the
direction it takes   On the contiary, he has infinitely
purified a barbarous tale which the taste of the age
authorized as a subject of dramatic representation
The scenes between the lower characters would have
been readily tolerated by a female audience in the
time of the first James, and although they must now
be passed over, we can hardly censure the poet for
not foreseeing the extreme delicacy of a later age
The offences chiefly consist of a few gioss words,
which no one but literary antiquarians will comprehend, and are purposely left without explanation.
Bearing in mind that the improprieties of language
above alluded to are faults of the age, not of the
poet's judgment, and that a similar apology may be
advanced for the choice of subject, the moral conveyed by 'Measuie for Measure' is of a deeply relig-

ious character. It exhibits in an outline of wonderful power how ineffective are the strongest resolutions against the insidious temptation of beauty, when they are not firmly strengthened and guarded by religion. The prayers of Angelo came from his lips, not from his heart, and he fell Isabella, on the contrary, is preserved by virtue grounded on religious faith. Her character is presented as nearly approaching perfection as is consistent with possible reality; and we rejoice that such a being should be snatched from the gloomy cloister to exercise her mild influence in a more useful station. The minor characters complete the picture of one of the chief phases of human life, the conflict of incontinence and chastity.'

17

HISTORICAL SUMMARY OF 'MUCH ADO ABOUT NOTHING.'

A STORY in some respects similar to this drama may be found in the fifth book of 'Orlando Furioso,' and likewise in the second book of 'Spenser's Fairy Queen,' but it is most probable that Shakespeare derived the principal incident of this comedy from a version of Belleforest, who copied the Italian novelist Bandello In the 22d tale of the first part of Bandello, and the 18th history of the third volume of Belleforest, a story is related, the events of which nearly resemble those attendant on the marriage of Claudio and Hero

As this play was printed in quarto in 1600, and is not mentioned by Meres in his list of Shakespeare's works published about the end of 1598, Mr Malone conjectures that the year 1600 may be accurately assigned as the time of its production It is reported to have been formerly known under the name of 'Benedick and Beatrice'

'This play,' says Steevens, 'may be justly said to contain two of the most sprightly characters that Shakespeare ever drew The wit, the humorist, the gentleman, and the soldier are combined in Benedick. It is to be lamented, indeed, that the first and most splendid of these distinctions is disgraced by unnecessary profaneness, for the goodness of his heart is hardly sufficient to atone for the license of his tongue. The too sarcastic levity which flashes out in the conversation of Beatrice may be excused on account of the

H. MERLE, PINX.

BENEDICK AND BEATRICE

Much Ado About Nothing, Act IV, Scene 1.

steadiness and friendship to her cousin, so apparent in her behavior, when she urges her lover to risk his life by a challenge to Claudio.' Heminge, the player, received on the 20th of May, 1613, the sum of £40 and £20 more as his Majesty's gratuity for exhibiting six plays at Hampton Court, among which was this comedy.

PERSONS REPRESENTED.

DON PEDRO, prince of Arragon
DON JOHN, his bastard brother
CLAUDIO, a young lord of Florence, favorite to Don Pedro.
BENEDICK, a young lord of Padua, favorite likewise of Don Pedro
LEONATO, governor of Messina.
ANTONIO, his brother.
BALTHAZAR, servant to Don Pedro
BORACHIO, } followers of Don John.
CONRADE, }
DOGBERRY, } two foolish officers.
VERGES, }
A SEXTON.
A FRIAR.
A BOY.

HERO, daughter to Leonato.
BEATRICE, niece to Leonato.
MARGARET, } gentlewomen attending on Hero.
URSULA, }

  Messengers, Watch, and Attendants.

    SCENE, Messina.

COMPENDIUM OF THE PLAY.   .

LEONATO, a gentleman of Messina, has an only daughter named Hero, whose beauty and accomplishments
captivate the affections of count Claudio, a favorite
of the prince then on a visit to her father, who
willingly gives his consent to a union so promising
In the meantime, Don John, a natural brother of
the prince, who has long viewed the elevation of
Claudio with a eye of jealousy, accuses the lady of
inconstancy, and, in confirmation of his assertion,
introduces his brother and his friend to her chamber
window at midnight : the artifice of an attendant
of Don John, named Borachio, who contrives to
address the waiting-maid stationed at the window by
the name of Hero, appears to leave no room for
doubt, and the enraged lover repudiates his affianced
bride at the very moment of the nuptials · Hero
faints, and, by the advice of the friar, a false report
of her death is circulated.   During the progress of
these events Borachio reveals the success of his
machinations to a fellow-servant whom he meets in
the street, and their conversation is overheard by
the watch, who convey the culprits to Leonato's
house, where a full confession is made by the repentant Borachio.   Claudio now entreats forgiveness from the insulted father, which is granted on
the condition of his union with a cousin of his
injured mistress, whose face he is not permitted to
behold till the completion of the marriage ceremony,
when his happiness is made perfect by finding himself the husband of the innocent Hero   A very
prominent part of this play is occupied with the

deception which is practised to betray Benedick and
Beatrice, two rival wits and professed marriage-
haters, into a mutual passion for each other, which
is at length accomplished, and they are both content
to renounce their prejudices against marriage Dogberry and Verges vary the notes of comedy by inimitable folly and pretension

It is not unworthy of remark, that Shakespeare's
muse appears to be more inventive in comedy than
in tragedy   In the latter, he has usually seized upon
some well-known story for his plot ; but his comedies
often are traceable to no source whatever, other than
his own wonderful genius, which seems to enjoy and
revel in wild 'rollicking fun and mad-cap diversion
In 'Much Ado About Nothing' he descends to broad
farce with our learned friend Dogberry, who assures
us that he is 'a wise fellow , and, which is more, an
officer , and, which is more, an householder , and,
which is more, as pretty a piece of flesh as any is in
Messina , and one that knows the law-go to , and a
rich fellow enough-go to , and a fellow that hath had
losses , and one that hath two gowns, and everything
handsome about him '   And his fellow-officer, the
feeble old Verges, who is, indeed, verging upon the
edge of the grave, but yet still clings to his parochial
dignity and gives his concurrence to the wise con-
clusions of his friend Dogberry, and thanks God that
he is 'as honest as any man living, that is an old man,
and no honester than he '   Then from this merriment
we are transported, without effort, to the interior of
the church, with its solemn sepulchral statuary, its
heraldic emblazonment, and its funereal-looking banners , where stands the monument which is supposed
to cover the corpse of Hero.   Here, at midnight, enters

the repentant Claudio, preceded by attendants with
dim-burning tapers, and sad music, to—

> 'Hang her an epitaph upon her tomb,
> And sing it to her bones.'

Indeed the serious portion of this play is exquisitely
conceived, the disgrace of the gentle Hero by her
lover's casting her off, and branding her with infamy,
even within the holy precincts of the church, where
he should have taken her to his heart, the astonishment of the guests, and that of Benedick, who exclaims —

> 'This looks not like a nuptial,'

and the hysterical answer of the terror-stricken girl
'True, O God!' would be altogether too tragic for
introduction into a comedy, but that the spectator
knows that the discovery of her innocence is already
made, although not yet revealed to her lover and her
friends   The agony and shame of her aged father
are painted in a manner worthy of our poet.

The discovery of the villany of Don John, who has
caused all the sorrow, is remarkable, Shakespeare
never omits an opportunity of illustrating his
favorite doctrine of the omnipresence of a jealous
Providence, which works through common means and
unsuspected channels, and returns to all men good for
good, evil for evil   It is most true

> 'Our indiscretion sometimes serves us well
> When our deep plots do pall; and that should teach us,
> There's a divinity that shapes our ends
> Rough-hew them how we will.'

For what the wisdom of Leonato, Claudio, and the

rest could not discover, was dragged from pitchy
darkness, and revealed in the full blaze of day by the
foolish and imbecile constables of the watch, Dogberry and his ancient friend Verges But the
chief interest of the play circles round Benedick
and Beatrice , it originally bore their names instead
of ‘ Much Ado,’ etc. , they have won for it its great
popularity , they love each other from the first, but
they do not know it , each of them has forsworn love
because they conceive it to be a cause of melancholy , the lady says she would ‘ rather hear a dog
bark at a cow than a man swear he loves her,’ while
Benedick tells us : ‘ I will not be sworn but love may
transform me to an oyster , but I’ll take my oath on
it, till he have made an oyster of me, he shall never
make me such a fool ’ It was a wild jest, and
worthy of the brain of Shakespeare, to bring two such
avowed infidels to love together, and entangle them
in the rose-linked meshes of Hymen , but this is
effected by the merry stratagem of making both believe
that each is the object of the concealed passion of the
other So that after Benedick has declared of his
cousin that —‘ She speaks poniards, and every word
stabs if her breath were as terrible as her termina-
tions, there were no living near her, she would infect
to the north star , I would not marry her though she
were endowed with all that Adam had left him
before he transgressed ,’ he offers her his hand and
heart, and loves her with as much warmth and sincerity, though certainly not with so much youthful
heart and passion, as the young ill-starred Romeo did
his mistress, Juliet Their mutual declaration of
affection is exquisite and in admirable keeping :—

Benedick—I protest I love thee.
Beatrice—Why, then, God forgive me!
Benedick—What offence, sweet Beatrice?
Beatrice—You have staid me in a happy hour;
   I was about to protest I loved you.

Many a lady might learn a winning lesson from this delightful frankness.

PAUL THUMANN, PINX.

OBERON AND TITANIA.

A Mid Summer-Nights Dream. Act IV. Scene I.

HISTORICAL SUMMARY OF 'A MIDSUMMER-NIGHT'S DREAM.'

THE Knight's Tale, in Chaucer, is supposed by Steevens to have been the prototype whence Shakespeare derived the leading features of this play the same writer conjectures that the doggerel verses of Bottom and his associates are nothing more than an extract from 'the boke of Perymus and Thesbye,' printed in 1562; while Mr Capell thinks our author indebted to a fantastical poem of Drayton, called Nymphidia, or the Court of Fairy, for his notions of those aerial beings

The title of this drama was probably suggested (like 'Twelfth Night' and 'The Winter's Tale') by the season of the year at which it was first represented no other ground, indeed, can be assigned for the name which it has received, since the action is distinctly pointed out as occurring on the night preceding May-day.

Of the 'Midsummer Night's-Dream' there are two editions in quarto, one printed for Thomas Fisher, the other for James Roberts, both in 1600. Neither of these editions deserves much praise for correctness Fisher is sometimes preferable, but Roberts was followed, though not without some variations, by Hemings and Condell, and they by all the folios that succeeded them

'Wild and fanciful as this play is,' says Dr. Johnson, 'all the parts in their various modes are well written, and give the kind of pleasure which the author designed Fairies in his time were much in fashion common tradition had made them familiar, and Spenser's poem had made them great.'

PERSONS REPRESENTED.

THESEUS, duke of Athens
EGEUS, father to Heimia
LYSANDER, } in love with Hermia
DEMETRIUS, }
PHILOSTRATE, master of the levels to Theseus.
QUINCE, the carpenter.
SNUG, the joiner.
BOTTOM, the weaver.
FLUTE, the bellows-mender.
SNOUT, the tinker.
STARVELING, the tailor.

HIPPOLYTA, } queen of the Amazons, betrothed to Theseus
HERMIA, daughter to Egeus, in love with Lysander.
HELENA, in love with Demetrius.
OBERON, king of the fairies.
TITANIA queen of the fairies
PUCK, or ROBIN-GOODFELLOW, a fairy.
PEAS-BLOSSOM, ⎤
COBWEB, ⎥
MOTH, ⎬ fairies.
MUSTARD-SEED, ⎦
PYRAMUS, ⎤
THISBE, ⎥
WALL, ⎬ characters in the interlude performed
MOONSHINE, ⎥   by the clowns.
LION, ⎦

Other fairies attending their king and queen
Attendants on Theseus and Hippolyta
SCENE, Athens, and a wood not far from it.

COMPENDIUM OF THE PLAY

OBERON, king of the fairies, requests his queen Titania
to bestow on him a favorite page to execute the
office of train-bearer, which she refusing, he, in
revenge, moistens her eyes during sleep with a
liquor, which possesses the singular property of
enamoring her of the first person she sees the
object which her eyes first encounter is an ignorant
Athenian weaver, named Bottom, who, together
with his associates, are preparing to represent a
play at the approaching nuptials of Theseus and
Hippolyta, when a waggish spirit of Oberon,
named Puck, covers Bottom with the head of an
ass,—a transformation which terrifies the rustic
swains, and fulfils the intention of his master, in
the dotage of his queen During this period, a
young couple, Lysander and Hermia, flying from a
cruel father, and the rigor of the Athenian laws,
which forbid their union, enter the enchanted wood,
whither they are pursued by Demetrius, whose suit
is favored by the father of the fugitive damsel, and
who is himself beloved by another lady following
him, named Helena, whom he treats with disdain
Oberon, in pity to Helena, commands Puck to
anoint the eyes of the churlish Demetrius with the
charmed liquor during sleep, but he by mistake
enchants Lysander Demetrius soon after becomes
the subject of the same operation, while Helena is
presented to each of the awakened lovers · the
object of their affections becomes now instantly
changed, and the hitherto favored Hermia is rejected by both, till Oberon at length disenchants
Lysander, restores the weaver to his pristine form,

and becomes reconciled to his queen The play concludes with the union of Hippolyta to Theseus, by whose mediation the father of Hermia consents to his daughter's marriage with Lysander, while Demetrius becomes the husband of Helena Schlegel says ''The different parts of the plot, the wedding of Theseus, the disagreement of Oberon and Titania, the flight of the two pair of lovers, and the theatrical operations of the mechanics, are so lightly and happily interwoven, that they seem necessary to each other for the formation of a whole Oberon is desirous of relieving the lovers from their perplexities, and greatly adds to them through the misapprehension of his servant, till he at last comes to the aid of their fruitless amorous pain, their inconstancy and jealousy, and restores fidelity to its old rights The extremes of fanciful and vulgar are united when the enchanted Titania awakes and falls in love with a coarse mechanic with an ass's head, who represents or rather disfigures the part of a tragical lover The droll wonder of the transmutation of Bottom is merely the translation of a metaphor in its literal sense ; but, in his behavior during the tender homage of the Fairy Queen, we have a most amusing proof how much the consciousness of such a head-dress heightens the effect of his usual folly Theseus and Hippolyta are, as it were, a splendid frame for the picture they take no part in the action, but appear with stately pomp The discourse of the hero and his Amazon, as they course through the forest with their noisy hunting train, works upon the imagination like the fresh breath of morning, before which the shapes of night disappear '

ARMADO AND JAQUENETTA.

Love's Labour's Lost.   Act I, Scene II.

HISTORICAL SUMMARY OF 'LOVE'S LABOR'S LOST '

No traces have yet been discovered of any novel or tale from which the incidents of this comedy have been borrowed The fable, however, does not appear to be a work of pure invention, and most probably is indebted for its origin to some romance, now no longer in existence The character of Holofernes is supposed to be the portrait of an individual , and some of his quotations have induced commentators to infer that John Florio, a pedantic teacher of Italian, was the object of the poet's satire

Malone conjectures that ' Love's Labor's Lost ' was first written in 1594, of which no exact transcript is preserved , for in the earliest edition which has hitherto been found of this play, namely that of 1598, it is said in the title page to be ' newly corrected and augmented,' with the farther information, that it had been ' presented before her highness the last Christmas ; ' facts, which show, that we are in possession, not of the first draught or edition of this comedy, but only of that copy which represents it as it was revived and improved for the entertainment of Queen Elizabeth in 1597 That this was one of Shakespeare's earliest essays in dramatic writing is clearly proved by the frequent rhymes, the imperfect versification, and the irregularity of the composition

' It must be confessed,' says Dr. Johnson, ' that

there are many passages in this play, mean, childish,
and vulgar, and some which ought not to have been
exhibited, as we are told they were, to a maiden queen
But there are scattered through the whole many sparks
of genius ; nor is there any play that has more evident
marks of the hand of Shakespeare '

PERSONS REPRESENTED.

FERDINAND, king of Navarre
BIRON,
LONGAVILLE, } lords attending on the king
DUMAIN,
BOYET,
MERCADE, } lords attending on the princess of France
DON ADRIANO DE ARMADO, a fantastical Spaniard
SIR NATHANIEL, a curate
HOLOFERNES, a schoolmaster
DULL, a constable
COSTARD, a clown
MOTH, page to Armado.
A FORESTER.

PRINCESS OF FRANCE
ROSALINE,
MARIA, } ladies attending on the princess
KATHARINE,
JAQUENETTA, a country wench

Officers and others, attendants on the king and princess

SCENE, Navarre.

COMPENDIUM OF THE PLAY.

FERDINAND, king of Navarre, having devoted himself
to the study of philosophy, prevails on three of his
courtiers, Biron, Longaville, and Dumain, to renounce
with him the pleasures of society, exacting an oath
from each, that for the space of three years they
would sedulously attend to the culture of their
minds, separate themselves entirely from the company of females, and practise the utmost simplicity
in their apparel and diet. At this critical juncture
the princess of France arrives at the palace of
Navarre on an embassy from the king, her father,
attended by three ladies in her train   her personal
charms and mental endowments soon make a powerful impression on the heart of the secluded monarch,
and he has the satisfaction of perceiving that his
fellow-students are not insensible to the attractions
of the ladies of the French court, but are equally
anxious with himself to obtain a dispensation of
their rash vow   An immediate prosecution of their
suit is now resolved on, which exposes them to the
raillery of their mistresses, who, after reproaching
the repentant devotees with their perjury, insist on
subjecting the permanence of their attachments to
the trial of a whole year, at the expiration of which
period they consent to become their wives   Costard,
a clown, and Moth, the page of Armado, are the
broad humorists of the play, assisted therein by
Jaquenetta, a country wench
Singer says, 'the scene in which the king and his
companions detect each other's breach of their mutual vow is capitally contrived   The discovery of

Biron's love-letter while rallying his friends, and the manner in which he extricates himself, by ridiculing the folly of the vow, are admirable.'

The grotesque characters, Don Adriano de Armado, a braggadochio, such as we find frequently in Italian comedies, Nathaniel the curate, and Holofernes, that prince of pedants (whom Warburton thought was intended as a ridicule of the resolute John Florio), with the humors of Costard the clown, are well contrasted with the sprightly wit of the principal characters in the play   It has been observed that 'Biron and Rosaline suffer much in comparison with Benedick and Beatrice,' and it must be confessed that there is some justice in the observation Yet Biron, 'that merry mad-cap lord,' is not over-rated in Rosaline's admirable character of him—

> 'A merrier man,
> Within the limit of becoming mirth,
> I never spent an hour's talk withal ;
> His eye begets occasion for his wit ;
> For every object that the one doth catch
> The other turns to a mirth-moving jest,—
> So sweet and voluble is his discourse '

There are other immortal characters in the play— Dull, the obtuse constable, on whom Shakespeare improved in Dogberry, and Moth, the page, that 'most acute juvenal,' are, both, original creations and thoroughly Shakespearian

FROM A PHOTOGRAPH BY N. SARONY.

THOMAS KEENE AS SHYLOCK.

Merchant of Venice Act I. Scene III.

HISTORICAL SUMMARY OF THE 'MER-CHANT OF VENICE.'

IT is generally believed that Shakespeare was in-debted to several sources for the materials of this admirable play. The story of the bond is taken from a tale in the Pecorone of Sir Giovanni, a Florentine novelist, who wrote in 1378, three years after the death of Boccace This book was probably known to our author through the medium of some translation no longer extant The coincidences between these pro-ductions are too striking to be overlooked Thus, the scene being laid at Venice , the residence of the lady at Belmont , the introduction of a person bound for the principal , the taking more or less than a pound of flesh, and the shedding of blood , together with the incident of the ring, are common to the novel and the play.

The choice of the caskets, in this comedy, is borrowed from chapter 49 of the English *Gesta Romanorum*, where three vessels are placed before the daughter of the king of Apulia for her choice, to prove whether she is worthy to receive the hand of the son of Anselmus, emperor of Rome The princess, after praying to God for assistance, rejects the gold and silver caskets, and chooses the leaden, which being opened, and found to be full of gold and precious stones, the emperor in-forms her that she has chosen as he wished, and immediately unites her to his son.

18

The love and elopement of Jessica and Lorenzo have been noticed by Mr Dunlop as bearing a similitude to the fourteenth tale of Massuccio di Salerno, who flourished about 1470 In that tale we meet with an avaricious father, a daughter carefully shut up, her elopement with her lover by the intervention of a servant, her robbing her father of his money, together with his grief on the discovery ;—a grief, divided equally between the loss of his daughter and the loss of his ducats.

Malone places the date of the composition of this play in 1593 It is mentioned by Meres in his list published in 1598 to be printed by James Roberts, if license were first had from the Lord Chamberlain. It was not printed by Roberts until 1600.

PERSONS REPRESENTED.

DUKE OF VENICE
PRINCE OF MOROCCO, } suitors to Portia.
PRINCE OF ARRAGON, }
ANTONIO, the merchant of Venice.
BASSANIO his friend.
SALANIO,
SALARINO, } friends to Antonio and Bassanio
GRATIANO,
LORENZO, in love with Jessica
SHYLOCK, a Jew
TUBAL, a Jew, his friend.
LAUNCELOT GOBBO, a clown, servant to Shylock.
OLD GOBBO, father to Launcelot.

SALERIO, a messenger from Venice.
LEONARDO, servant to Bassanio
BALTHAZAR, } servants to Portia.
STEPHANO,

PORTIA, a rich heiress
NERISSA, her waiting-maid
JESSICA, daughter to Shylock

Magnificoes of Venice, Officers of the court of justice,
Jailer, Servants, and other Attendants.

SCENE, partly at Venice, and partly at Belmont, the
country-seat of Portia

COMPENDIUM OF THE PLAY.

A RICH and beautiful heiress residing at Belmont,
named Portia, is compelled by the will of her deceased
father to subject every suitor to the choice, by random
guess, of a golden, silver, or leaden casket . in the latter is enclosed a portrait of the lady, who is to become
the wife of its fortunate selector Bassanio, a young
Venetian gentleman, at length obtains the prize, and
is scarcely united to his bride, when he receives intelligence from Venice that his dear friend Antonio, from
whose liberality he has procured the means of prose-
cuting his suit, is completely ruined ; and that a bond,
which he has executed with a Jew for the payment
of a sum of money within a certain period, on forfeit-

ure of a pound of flesh nearest his heart, is now demanded by his inexorable creditor. After receiving a ring from his bride with professions of constancy, Bassanio flies to the relief of his patron the lady, in the meantime, procures letters of recommendation from an eminent jurist, and, in the disguise of a doctor of laws, is introduced to the duke, as a person well qualified to decide the cause pending between the merchant and the Jew; and at length, by her ingenuity, the unfortunate debtor is delivered from his savage persecutor The disguised lawyer persists in refusing all pecuniary recompense, but entreats from Bassanio the ring which she had presented to him at his departure, which he reluctantly yields the same expedient is successfully tried by the waiting-maid, who is the wife of Gratiano, disguised as a lawyer's clerk The lady and her attendant now hasten home, and, on the arrival of their husbands, amuse themselves with witnessing their confusion at the loss of their love tokens, till the stratagem is at length fully explained The remainder of this play is occupied with the elopement of Jessica, the daughter of the Jew, with a young man named Lorenzo, who procures from his father-in-law the reversion of his whole property Gratiano is the bright, light-hearted friend of Antonio and Bassanio, who weds Nerissa Shylock is not more cruel than his age; for Antonio, honest merchant as he is, would have converted the Jews to Christianity by means of the inquisition; and when Shylock is every way defeated and humbled, insists on his apostatizing from his religious faith, or he will take from him the remaining moiety of his wealth. We do not participate largely in the general sympathy for Antonio; he is full of the prejudices of conventionality, rather dogmatic, melan-

choly without a cause, and of an unsocial nature The
rattling Gratiano gives him wholesome advice, and although Antonio pretends to despise it, the lively jester
is the wiser of the two Antonio is a bad political
economist, he lends money without interest, because he
does not understand its value as a commodity in mer-
chandise, as well as its use as a medium of exchange,
but he has no right to rail on Shylock, because he declines to follow a profitless and erroneous example
He had gratified his hate to the Jew by many mean
and insolent provocations, altogether unworthy of the
conduct of a Venetian gentleman; and the act of
spitting upon the bread of the Israelite was little short
of absolute ruffianism Still the amiable Antonio justifies this conduct, and says he is likely to repeat it
'After this,' as Mr Hazlitt well remarks, 'the appeal
to the Jew's mercy, as if there were any common
principle of right and wrong between them, is the
rankest hypocrisy, or the blindest prejudice' Mrs
Jamieson (a delightful and very acute writer) is angry
with Hazlitt because he thinks Portia a clever woman,
and because he says she has a degree of affectation
about her which is not usual in Shakespeare's representation of women She exclaims—'Portia clever!
why the word clever implies something common-place,
inasmuch as it speaks the presence of the active and
perceptive, with a deficiency of the feeling and reflect-
ive powers.' 'Portia,' she eloquently continues,
' hangs beside the terrible inexorable Jew, the brilliant
lights of her character set off by the shadowy power
of his, like a magnificent beauty-breathing Titian by
the side of a gorgeous Rembrandt' Notwithstanding
Mrs Jamieson's appeal in behalf of Portia, we are
somewhat inclined to side with Hazlitt in his estimate

of the character, she is too quick and sarcastic, and a
little too forward   Many of her speeches are very
beautiful, and all of them are evidence that she is a
woman of great intellect   Nerissa is a pert imitator of
her mistress—a copy in water-colors of a fine oil painting   Jessica is not an amiable creation ; she runs away
from her father to marry one of a race he detests,
this is an offence, but still, under the peculiar circumstances, not an unforgivable one   but she robs her
father, and wantonly wastes the proceeds of her dishonesty.   She has no compunction in leaving her home
thus stealthily, on the contrary, her last thought before quitting it is, that she has not helped herself sufficiently to her father's stores   There is a selfishness
about this that is disgusting, but the usurer's love of
money descended to his offspring, and that which is
greedily accumulated by the father is idly dissipated
by the daughter   The trial scene is a masterpiece of
dramatic construction, a play in itself, with every character perfectly developed   Shylock defends his own
cause, and urges his claim with consummate skill ; he
stands like a rock, unshaken by the waves of argument
which repeatedly dash against him   His answers are
admirable, elated by a feeling of assured success—tri-
umphing in the anticipated death of his enemy whom
he contemplates offering as a sacrifice to the insulted
genius of his people, he at first replies in a bantering
vein—he'll not answer—it is his humor   but when the
duke appeals to his religious feelings, he enters freely
into argument—denies that he falls within the censure
of the sacred law—he has as much right to a pound
of the body of Antonio. which is his by purchase, as
they have to the bodies of their domestic slaves   Shylock has the best of the argument, and he feels that

he has. The duke cannot answer him, but talks about dismissing the court, when Portia opportunely arrives. At her appearance—taking her for a youth, and, therefore, an inexperienced lawyer—he regards her with a smile of triumph—he is the more certain of his revenge Already, in imagination, does he see the once haughty, scoffing merchant quivering and fainting beneath his weapon Gratiano utters a violent invective against him he answers, with derisive scorn and a bitter wit—

> ' Till thou can'st rail the seal from off my bond,
> Thou but offend'st thy lungs to speak so loud.'

Portia then appeals to his sense of humanity, but his heart is closed, he is offered thrice his money, but avarice is overpowered and swallowed up by a gigantic desire of revenge Portia makes one final attempt to arouse his feelings,—he will at least have at hand a surgeon, lest Antonio should bleed to death, but he cannot find it so nominated in the bond, and he adheres to the strict letter of the law It is now that our feelings turn against the Jew, a revenge so implacable seems fiendish, we forget his wrongs, and our sympathy is lost to him He demands judgment, and flourishing his knife, exclaims to his intended victim, in a voice of vindictive malice, ' Come, prepare ' The scale is now turned, he is told to cut off the pound of flesh, but, adds Portia—

> ' This bond doth give thee here no jot of blood,' etc.

Shylock at once perceives himself defeated ruined, and triumphed over, his wealth is confiscated and his life is ostentatiously pardoned, but on such conditions,

that in the agony of his soul, he solicits them to take
that too, and finally, with a bitter, heart-broken sigh,
he totters from the court, to hide his sorrow in his
lonely and deserted house, a childless, ruined man.
We hear no more of Shylock, but the interest is well
sustained during the remaining act, and as poetry, it
is perhaps superior to the rest of the play, it is like a
strain of exquisite melody to soothe the ruffled spirit
of the spectator after the excitement of the trial.   The
light buffoon of the play is Launcelot Gobbo   It is as
impossible for Shakespeare to get along without a
clown, as for a circus of the present day to omit that
amusing feature of the performance

FROM A PHOTOGRAPH BY DOWNEY.

MARY ANDERSON AS ROSALIND.

As You Like It. Act II. Scene IV.

HISTORICAL SUMMARY OF 'AS YOU LIKE IT '

THE plot of this beautiful and romantic comedy has been attributed by Dr Grey and Mr Upton to the Coke's Tale of Gamelyn, erroneously called Chaucer's , but no printed edition of that work made its appearance till near a century after the death of our author, who contented himself with borrowing his story from a novel, or rather pastoral romance, entitled ' Euphues' Golden Legacy,' written in a very fantastical style by Dr Thomas Lodge, and by him first published in 1590 In addition to the fable, which is pretty exactly followed, the outlines of the principal characters may be traced in the novel, with the exception of Jaques, Touchstone, and Audrey, who are generally admitted to be the creation of the poet

The first publication of 'As You Like It' appears to have been the folio of 1623 It is supposed by Malone to have been written after 1596, and before 1600. We learn by tradition that Shakespeare himself performed the part of Adam.

'Of this play,' writes Dr Johnson, 'the fable is wild and pleasing. I know not how the ladies will approve the facility with which both Rosalind and Celia give away their hearts To Celia much may be forgiven for the heroism of her friendship The character of Jaques is one of force and originality The comic dialogue is very sprightly, with less mixture of

low buffoonery than in some other plays, and the
graver part is elegant and harmonious   By hastening
to the end of his work, Shakespeare suppressed the
dialogue between the usurper and the hermit, and lost
an opportunity of exhibiting a moral lesson, in which
he might have found matter worthy of his highest
powers.'

PERSONS REPRESENTED

DUKE, living in exile

FREDERICK, brother to the Duke, and usurper of his
    dominions

AMIENS, }
JAQUES, } lords attending upon the Duke in his ban-
    ishment

LE BEAU, a courtier attending upon Frederick.

CHARLES, his wrestler

OLIVER, }
ORLANDO, } sons of Sir Rowland de Bois

ADAM, }
DENNIS, } servants to Oliver

TOUCHSTONE, a clown

SIR OLIVER MAR-TEXT, a vicar

CORIN, }
SYLVIUS, } shepherds

WILLIAM, a country fellow, in love with Audrey.

A person representing HYMEN

ROSALIND, daughter to the banished Duke

CELIA, daughter to Frederick

FROM A PHOTOGRAPH BY FALK.

MAURICE BARRYMORE AS ORLANDO.

As You Like It. Act III. Scene II.

PHEBE, a shepherdess
AUDREY, a country wench

Lords belonging to the two Dukes; Pages, Foresters,
and other Attendants

The SCENE lies, first, near Oliver's house, afterwards,
partly in the usurper's court, and partly
in the forest of Arden

COMPENDIUM OF THE PLAY.

A DUKE of France, being dispossessed of his domin-
ions by Frederick, his younger brother, retires to the
forest of Arden with a few faithful adherents, leaving
behind him his daughter Rosalind, who is detained at
the court of the usurper to be a companion to her
cousin Celia While here, Rosalind becomes enamored
of young Orlando, son of Sir Roland de Bois, the old
duke's friend, who signalizes himself in wrestling before
the court The accomplishments and popularity of
Rosalind soon however, excite the apprehensions of
her uncle, who banishes her from his territories the
affection of Celia prompts her to accompany her kins-
woman, and she makes her escape in the disguise of a
shepherdess, while Rosalind assumes the habit of a
man Arrived at the forest of Arden, the two friends
purchase a house and grounds, where they reside for
some time as brother and sister here they are agree-
ably surprised at the presence of Orlando, who, in order to guard his life from the machinations of Oliver,

his elder brother, is compelled to join the company of
the banished Duke Rosalind, after, by delightful
strategy, satisfying herself of the attachment of her
lover, and the willingness of her father to consent to
their union, resumes her female apparel, and bestows
her hand on Orlando, while Celia becomes the wife of
the repentant Oliver, whose life is preserved from the
fury of a lion by the bravery of his injured brother
In the meantime Duke Frederick, jealous of the in-
creasing number of his opponents, arrives with a large
army for the purpose of exterminating them on the
skirts of the forest he is encountered by an old hermit,
who dissuades him from the prosecution of his cruel
enterprise Struck with remorse, he voluntarily re-
signs his dukedom, and retires from the world,
while the exiles are reinstated in their former
dignities The character of Jaques is natural and
well preserved—one of the most pleasant philoso-
phers the world has ever seen Touchstone is the
most intellectual of the fools of Shakespeare , he is a
great lover of argument , there is no broad farcical
fun about him, but a grave humor which is admirable He is a moral teacher, too, in his way, and regrets
‘ that fools may not speak wisely what wise men do
foolishly ’ Some of his sayings are aphorisms of considerable wisdom, as, ‘ Rich honesty dwells like a
miser, sir, in a poor house ; as your pearl in your foul
oyster , ’ and ‘ Your *If* is your only peacemaker;
much virtue in an *If* ’ In the introduction of Sir
Oliver Mar-text (a character seldom played), our poet
indulges in a sly hit against the Puritan and itinerant
ministers, whom he appears to have regarded with
aversion The concluding observation of the curate
stamps him as a man not properly qualified for the

clerical profession   Audrey is a country lass, as ignorant as might be supposed from a life of so isolated a
nature, but there is something really winning in the
poor girl's natural simplicity   Touchstone, regretting
her want of an appreciative understanding of his humorous sallies, wishes that the gods had made her poetical, to which she replies   'I do not know what poetical is , is it honest in deed and word ?   Is it a true
thing? '   This character is often misunderstood upon
the stage, being represented as a coarse country gawky ,
a little consideration of the poet will show that she is
an artless, comely peasant-girl, ignorant enough, but
attractive from her fresh rural simplicity and unre-
served sincerity.

HISTORICAL SUMMARY OF 'ALL'S WELL THAT ENDS WELL'

THE fable of this comedy is taken from a novel, of which Boccace is the original author; but which was immediately derived by Shakespeare from the tale of Giletta of Narbonne, in the first volume of William Painter's 'Palace of Pleasure,' printed at London in 1566   To this novel, however, the poet was only indebted for the leading features of the more serious parts of his drama   the comic characters, and especially that of Parolles, appear to be entirely of his own formation

A supposed allusion to the fanaticism of the Puritans induced Malone to assign the date of 1606 to the composition of this play , but the many passages of rhyme scattered throughout seem to mark it as an earlier production   In 1598 Meres refers to a play of Shakespeare, called 'Love's Labor Wonne,' which very accurately applies to this, but to no other of our author's productions . we have reason therefore to conclude that it was intended as a counter-title to 'Love's Labor's Lost ,' and that the present proverbial appellation was suggested in consequence of the adage itself being found in the body of the play

'This play,' says Dr Johnson, ' has many delightful and some happy characters, though not new, nor produced by any deep knowledge of human nature. Parolles is a boaster and a coward, such as has always

F.PECHT.PINX.

BERTRAM AND THE COUNTESS [FAREWELL]

All's Well that Ends Well. Act I., Scene I.

been the sport of the stage , but perhaps never raised more laughter or contempt than in the hands of Shakespeare   I cannot reconcile my heart to Bertram ; a man noble without generosity, and young without truth · who marries Helena as a coward, and leaves her as a profligate   when she is dead by his unkindness, sneaks home to a second marriage , is accused by a woman whom he has wronged , defends himself by falsehood ; and is dismissed to happiness. '

PERSONS REPRESENTED.

KING OF FRANCE
DUKE OF FLORENCE
BERTRAM, count of Rousillon.
LAFEU, an old lord
PAROLLES, a follower of Bertram.
Several young French Lords, that serve with Bertram
    in the Florentine war
STEWARD, ⎫
CLOWN,   ⎬ servants to the countess of Rousillon.
A PAGE, ⎭

COUNTESS OF ROUSILLON, mother to Bertram.
HELENA, a gentlewoman protected by the countess.
An old WIDOW of Florence
DIANA, daughter to the widow.
VIOLENTA, ⎫
MARIANA, ⎬ neighbors and friends to the widow.
    Lords attending on the king ; Officers, Soldiers, etc.,
        French and Florentine.
    SCENE, partly in France and partly in Tuscany.

COMPENDIUM OF THE PLAY.

HELENA, the daughter of a celebrated physician, conceives a violent attachment to Bertram, count of Rousillon, who on the death of his father repairs to Paris, as a ward of the king of France, at this time languishing under the influence of a distemper which has been pronounced incurable   Directed by the medical knowledge she has received from her father, Helena procures an audience of the monarch, and undertakes to effect his cure, on condition of choosing for herself a husband, with reservation only of the royal family   The king is restored to health, and the lady fixes her choice on Bertram   Unable to resist, the young count reluctantly consents to the nuptials, which are no sooner performed, than he dismisses his bride to her home, and sets out for Florence, whence he sends her a letter intimating his determination of never cohabiting with her till (what he considers to be an impossibility) she obtains a ring which he wears on his finger, and is pregnant by him   The receipt of this epistle induces Helena to quit the castle of Rousillon, and proceed to Italy, where she hears of her husband's unsuccessful attempts on the chastity of a widow's daughter, on whom she prevails to pretend to accede to his solicitations, and Helena is afterwards introduced in her stead to the bed of Bertram, and there contrives to exchange rings with him   Soon after Bertram, having received intelligence of the death of Helena, returns to France, and is reconciled to the king, who is

about to consent to his union with the daughter of a
favorite courtier, when he detects a ring in his possession, which he had formerly presented to Helena, who
had contrived to place it on her husband's finger during his supposed assignation with his Italian mistress
Failing to give any satisfactory account of the means
by which he obtained it, he is suspected of having
murdered his wife, when Helena appears, satisfies her
husband of the fulfilment of his requisitions, and is publicly acknowledged by the repentant Bertram   We
could have wished that the long discussion between
Parolles and Helena in the first act had been given to
some other character , it profanes the otherwise delicate
modesty of her nature, which is on no other occasion
overstepped or laid aside , even in her strange plan to
obtain the affections of her husband   This coarse dialogue, witty and ingenious as it is, would have been
better omitted , it was one of Shakespeare's numerous
concessions to the sensuality of his audiences   The
Countess, mother of Bertram, is a highly interesting
character , Shakespeare invests all his matious with
dignity , he is no ungallant poet who represents the
young only as attractive   The amiability and wisdom
of the Countess win our admiration, and her directions
to her son on his leaving her for the court, though
brief, may be justly placed in comparison with Polonius's sage and excellent advice to Laertes on a similar
occasion.   The king is a philosophical invalid, who utters many valuable moral truths , his expostulation
with Bertram on his pride of birth is a piece of powerful reasoning.   It is equally true as strange that, despite our lofty pretensions and cherished ancestral dignities, our blood poured altogether 'would quite con-
found distinction.'   Parolles is the great comic crea-
19

tion of the piece, a fop, a fool, a liar, a braggart, and
every way a knave, and yet, with all these vices, amusing enough He is too contemptible for anger; we
almost pity him when he is discovered and disgraced,
and even when he is exposed to the unmerciful raillery
of the jovial old Lord Lafeu, who says 'there can be
no kernel in this light nut, the soul of this man is his
clothes ' His adventure in search of the lost drum,
which he swears he will recover or perish in attempting
to do so, and then goes out for a walk at night to de-
vise some account of his expedition, is a piece of admirable comedy But his being taken prisoner by his
own companions (who suspect his cowardice), blind-
folded and made to confess to them the secrets of their
own camp, is irresistibly amusing, equal in broad fun
to Falstaff's midnight adventure at Gadshill But Parolles cannot extricate himself from a difficulty with
the same dexterity that is evinced by the jovial fat
knight, once discovered he is disgraced forever, and
he resolves to give up military pretensions and live
'safest in shame ' He turns parasite and gets his
bread by flattery In this new capacity he shows great
dexterity, and when he enters in soiled and ragged attire, he propitiates the old Lord Lafeu in his favor by
a delicate compliment, 'O my good Lord, you were
the first that found me,' that is, your strong sense
and discernment first discovered me to be a braggart
and no soldier The shrewd old noble is flattered into
compassion, and exclaims 'Though you are a fool
and a knave, you shall eat go to, follow '

Monsieur Lavatch, the clown, with his answer that
suits all questions, adds to the comic interest of the
play, and may fairly take rank with Touchstone and
Feste for humor and equivocating wit

In noticing the beauties of this comedy, the scene where the young Count Bertram woos Diana to yield to his impetuous and unlawful love should not be forgotten; a finer lesson on maiden purity was never preached, a holier caution to young and susceptible beauty never fell from the lips of moralist or sage.

HISTORICAL SUMMARY OF THE 'TAMING
OF THE SHREW '

NOTHING appears to invalidate the conclusion of
Malone that this was one of Shakespeare's earlier
plays, although Warburton and Farmer have disputed
its authenticity It abounds with the doggerel measure
and tedious play on words, so observable in 'The
Comedy of Errors,' and 'Love's Labor's Lost,' which
Shakespeare took occasion to condemn in one of his
subsequent comedies The year 1596 is the probable
date of its production, since in 1594, an old play, on
which the present drama is supposed to be founded,
was entered at Stationers' Hall, entitled 'Taming of a
Shrew,' which is attributed to the pen of George Peele
or Robert Greene The plots of these two pieces are
found to be essentially the same.

The story of Lucentio, and his artifice to obtain the
hand of Bianca, is formed on a comedy of George
Gascoigne, from the Italian of Ariosto, called 'Supposes,' which was performed by the gentlemen of
Gray's Inn in 1566 , and the Induction is borrowed
from Goulart's *Histoires Admirables de nôtre Temps*.
translated from the Latin of Heuterus, who relates a
similar delusion, which was practised on the credulity
of a poor artisan at Brussels by Philip the Good, duke
of Burgundy.

(66)

E.GRUTZNER, PINX.

KATHARINA AND PETRUCHIO.

The Taming of the Shrew, Act IV, Scene I.

PERSONS REPRESENTED.

A LORD.

CHRISTOPHER SLY, a drunken tinker
Hostess, Page, Players, Huntsmen,
   and other servants attending on the } Persons in the
   lord. Induction.

BAPTISTA, a rich gentleman of Padua

VINCENTIO, an old gentleman of Pisa.

LUCENTIO, son to Vincentio, in love with Bianca

PETRUCHIO, a gentleman of Verona, a suitor to
   Katharina

GREMIO,
HORTENSIO, } suitors to Bianca.

TRANIO,
BIONDELLO, } servants to Lucentio

GRUMIO,
CURTIS, } servants to Petruchio

PEDANT, an old fellow set up to personate Vincentio

KATHARINA, the shrew,
BIANCA, her sister, } daughters to Baptista.
WIDOW.

Tailor, Haberdasher, and Servants attending on Baptista and Petruchio

SCENE, sometimes in Padua , and sometimes in Petruchio's house in the country.

COMPENDIUM OF THE PLAY.

A NOBLEMAN, returning from the chase, finds an ignorant tinker, named Sly, lying on the bench of an alehouse, dead-drunk, and causes him to be conveyed home, laid on one of his richest beds, and arrayed in the most costly apparel When the drunkard awakes, he is surrounded by attendants, who succeed in persuading him that he is a nobleman, who for many years has been laboring under mental delusion The conviction of Sly that he is 'a lord indeed' is succeeded by the introduction of a company of players, who entertain him with the representation of a comedy, of which the following is a brief outline · A citizen of Padua, named Baptista, the father of Katharina and Bianca, refuses to listen to the numerous admirers of the latter till after the marriage of her elder sister, whose violence of temper effectually deters all suitors; and the lovers of Bianca are compelled to resort to the expedient of procuring a husband for Katharina, which they accomplish, in the person of Petruchio. By a rough and singular method of courtship the shrew is won, and at length tamed by a perseverance in the same course of treatment. In the meantime, Lucentio, a young gentleman of Pisa, introduces himself to Bianca in the disguise of a classical tutor, and succeeds in obtaining her hand by the intervention of his servant Tranio, who assumes the name and apparel of his master in order to forward his designs The presence of Lucentio's father becomes necessary, and Tranio devises the scheme of engaging a schoolmaster to represent him. At this critical juncture the real father unexpectedly arrives, and encounters his son's servant in his master's clothes Tranio impudently disclaims all knowledge of his master's father, who is about to be committed to jail as an impostor, when his son enters with his bride, and a reconciliation is speedily effected Schlegel thinks that the latter part of Shakespeare's play of 'Taming of a Shrew' has been lost, or that the remarks of the tinker during the progress of the play were left to the judgment of the actor, though he also admits that it is unlikely that the poet should have left to chance the conclusion of that which he had so carefully commenced The character of Sly in the introduction is drawn with a broad pencil, and in a style of the richest humor, he is very sceptical of the truth and reality of his newly acquired rank, and asks incredulously—'am I not Christopher Sly, old Sly's son of Burton-heath , by birth, a pedlar , by education, a card-maker , by transmutation, a bear-herd, and now, by present profession, a tinker!' To dissipate his doubts, his deceivers call in the aid of music, and description in language exquisitely glowing, of the pleasures which await him They describe his horses, hawks, and hounds, his pictures :

> ' Adonis, painted by a running brook ,
> And Cytherea all in sedges hid ,
> Which seem to move and wanton with her breath,
> Even as the waving sedges play with wind '

And lastly his wife, whom they describe as—

> ' A lady far more beautiful
> Than any woman in this waning age.'

The poor tinker is bewildered and convinced, and determines to celebrate, what he supposes to be his re-

turn to reason, with 'a pot o' the smallest ale' In
the play itself, Petruchio and Katharina are eminently Shakespearian creations Petruchio, Benedick,
and Mercutio, etc., are a class of characters peculiar
to our poet, and which could only have been written
by a man with a natural cheerfulness and love of humanity In drawing the character of Katharina,
Shakespeare has pictured a woman naturally of a
kind though irritable disposition, made a complete
scold by early indulgence and a bad education Petruchio undertakes to re-educate her, and he does so with
a happy effect the virago becomes a gentle and obe-
dient wife. Her lecture, after she has been tamed,
in the banquet scene, to her sister and the widow,
on the duty which a woman owes her husband, is
a fine moral sermon, dressed in language of the lofti-
est poetry Beaumont and Fletcher's comedy of 'The
Woman's Prize, or, the Tamer Tam'd,' is a continuation of the 'Taming of the Shrew,' and in it Petruchio is in his turn subdued by a second wife.

G. MAX, PINX.

FLORIZEL AND PERDITA.

The Winters Tale, Act IV. Scene III.

HISTORICAL SUMMARY OF 'THE WINTER'S TALE'

THE story of this play is taken from Robert Greene's 'Pleasant History of Dorastus and Fawnia,' which was published in 1588. Shakespeare has, however, changed the names of the characters, and added the parts of Antigonus, Paulina. and Autolycus from his own invention

'The Winter's Tale' was not entered on the Stationers' books, or printed till 1623, while we learn from Vertue's manuscripts that it was acted at court in 1613. Malone attributes the composition to the year 1611, but Lord Orford assigns to it a much earlier date, and conjectures that it was written during the lifetime of Elizabeth, and that it was intended as an indirect apology for Anne Boleyn, in which light it might be considered as a sequel to 'King Henry VIII'

Much censure has been cast on our author by Dryden and Pope for his disregard of the classical unities, which are nowhere so daringly violated as in this production, where we meet with a young woman becoming a bride, who, but a few minutes before, had been deposited on the sea-shore, a new-born infant.

Schlegel has observed of this drama that its title is happily adapted to its subject, being 'one of those tales which are peculiarly calculated to beguile the dreary leisure of a long winter evening, which is even attractive and intelligible to childhood, and which, animated by fervent truth in the delineation of character and passion, invested with the decoration of a poetry

(71)

lowering itself, as it were, to the simplicity of the subject, transport even manhood back to the golden age of imagination.'

PERSONS REPRESENTED

LEONTES, king of Sicilia
MAMILLIUS, his son
CAMILLO,
ANTIGONUS,
CLEOMENES, } Sicilian lords.
DION,
Another Sicilian Lord.
ROGERO, a Sicilian gentleman.
An Attendant on the young prince Mamillius.
Officers of a court of judicature.
POLIXENES, king of Bohemia.
FLORIZEL, his son
ARCHIDAMUS, a Bohemian lord.
A MARINER.
JAILER.
An old SHEPHERD, reputed father of Perdita.
CLOWN, his son
Servant to the old Shepherd.
AUTOLYCUS, a rogue
TIME, as chorus

HERMIONE, queen to Leontes
PERDITA, daughter to Leontes and Hermione.
PAULINA, wife to Antigonus
EMILIA, a lady,
Two other Ladies, } attending the queen

MOPSA, } shepherdesses.
DORCAS, }

Lords, Ladies and Attendants; Satyrs for a dance;
Shepherds, Shepherdesses, Guards, etc

SCENE, sometimes in Sicilia , sometimes in Bohemia.

COMPENDIUM OF THE PLAY.

POLIXENES, king of Bohemia, during a visit to his
friend Leontes, king of Sicily, awakens the jealousy of
his host, who unjustly suspects him of an intrigue
with his wife Hermione, and endeavors to prevail on a
courtier, named Camillo, to poison his guest instead,
however, of complying with his request, Camillo informs the unsuspecting monarch of his danger, and
accompanies him in his flight to Bohemia Leontes
now vents his rage on the innocent Hermione, who is
debarred from the society of her son, and confined in
prison, where she is delivered of a daughter named
Perdita, who is considered by Leontes as spurious,
and ordered to be exposed for death Antigonus, to
whose custody the infant is committed, reaches the
Bohemian territories, and during his progress is stran-
gled by a bear, while the child is found by a poor
shepherd, who rears it as his own In the meantime,
the character of Hermione is completely vindicated by
the answer of the oracle of Delphi, which informs Leontes that he shall want an heir to his kingdom till
the lost infant is found , and in confirmation of its

truth, his son suddenly expires immediately after the arrival of the commissioners The spirits of the queen are unable to sustain this last shock, she nearly dies, and the intelligence of her death is soon after conveyed to her repentant husband At the age of sixteen, Perdita captivates the affections of Florizel, the son of Polixenes, who contrives to escape from Bohemia with his affianced bride, and reaches the coast of Sicily, whither he is pursued by his enraged father the apparel and jewels, which were found with the infant at the time of its exposure, are now produced by the shepherd, and Perdita is recognized as the daughter of Leontes, and bestowed in marriage on her lover. Paulina, the widow of Antigonus, invites her master and his guests to inspect a statue of Hermione, which excites unbounded admiration as a triumph of art, when the supposed marble becomes animated, and Leontes recovers his amiable wife, who had in retirement awaited the fulfilment of the oracle Antolycus, the rogue, and the young shepherd and his two sweethearts, Mopsa and Dorcas, are a source of pleasant relief and merriment

Henry Tyrrell says · Shakespeare has been much censured on account of his utter disregard of the unities of time and place in this play, and for his anachronisms and geographical errors Sixteen years elapse between the third and fourth acts, which circumstance so shocked Dryden that, speaking of this and some other productions of Shakespeare, he said they 'were either grounded on impossibilities, or so meanly written, that the comedy neither caused your mirth nor the serious part your concernment '

The master-spirit of the drama is not to be measured with a foot-rule and bound down by frigid regulations, which every powerful imagination makes use of only so far as they are consistent with and favorable to his own design Mr Steevens has justly remarked that Shakespeare 'was not ignorant of these rules, but disregarded them '

With respect to the geographical error of making Bohemia a sea-bounded country, and opening a water communication between it and Sicilia, the poet doubtless erred from ignorance Greene, from whose story of 'Pandosta' he had borrowed the subject, had previously fallen into the same error, and Shakespeare has copied it without examination We are willing to grant this freely, but it takes nothing from the exquisite beauty of the play, it is none the less one of the finest comedies in existence although it contains a geographical error. It is the critic's duty to point out such literal imperfections, that they might not mislead the uninformed, but it betrays a pert and hasty judgment, when, presuming on the existence of such errors, he proceeds to condemn the work It is as if a man finding among many precious pearls a few worthless pebbles should condemn them all as valueless

Leontes is justly punished for his suspicion, his infant and dearly loved son pines and dies in consequence of his mother's disgrace, his daughter is bred up by rude shepherds at a distance from her stricken father, and his queen lost to him for a period of sixteen years, during which he bitterly reproaches himself as the cause of her supposed death His remorse is not diminished by time, when the long separation is about to cease, and Paulina reminds him of the perfections of the woman he had killed, he answers mournfully.

> 'She I kill'd? I did so; but thou strik'st me
> Sorely, to say I did.'

Shakespeare had the materials of a tragedy in his hand, had he been so disposed to treat the subject, but he chose to make it, like life, a mingled yarn of good and evil, smiles and tears, and the sense of gloom produced by the sad effects of Leontes' jealousy is dissipated by the charm of rustic, yet still majestic, beauty, which surrounds Perdita, as the queen of the rural feast, distributing flowers and discoursing sweetly on their names and nature, by the quaint humor of the rogue, Autolycus, who, like his namesake, the son of Mercury, is 'a snapper up of unconsidered trifles,' and by the hearty merriment of the young shepherd and his two sweethearts, Mopsa and Dorcas The court and the cottage are brought closely together, and while suspicion and remorse abide with princes, cheerfulness and mirth dwell with peasants

All throughout this play the language is in the poet's most mature and perfect style, it is profuse in beauty, wanton and luxuriant in exquisite imaginations and aphorisms of deep wisdom How admirable is Paulina's taunt to the passionate monarch, when he threatens to condemn her to the stake.

> ' I care not,
> It is an heretic that makes the fire,
> Not she which burns in it '

And for beauty, the whole of the third scene of the fourth act may be quoted as being almost without a parallel. The concluding scene also, where the supposed statue of Hermione is exhibited, and where, at the word of Paulina, it assumes animation, and the still living queen is restored to the embraces of her repentant husband, and her daughter, who had been estranged from her from the first hour of her birth, is an admirable and touching invention of Shakespeare's own inspiration.

FROM A PHOTOGRAPH BY N. SARONY.

ROBSON AND CRANE AS THE TWO DROMIOS.

Comedy of Errors, Act V., Scene I.

HISTORICAL SUMMARY OF THE 'COMEDY OF ERRORS.'

SHAKESPEARE appears to have taken the general plan of this comedy from a translation of the 'Menæchmi of Plautus,' by W. W., i e (according to Wood), William Warner, in 1595, whose version of the argument is as follows —

> 'Two twinne-borne sons a Sicill marchant had,
>   Menechmus one, and Sosicles the other
> The first his father lost, a little lad,
>   The grandsire namde the latter like his brother.
> This, growne a man, long travell tooke to seeke
>   His brother, and to Epidamnum came,
> Where th' other dwelt inricht, and him so like,
>   That citizens there take him for the same;
> Father, wife, neighbours, each mistaking either,
>   Much pleasant error, ere they meete togither.'

Perhaps the last of these lines suggested to Shakespeare the title for his piece

'In this play,' says Mr. Steevens, 'we find more intricacy of plot than distinction of character; and our attention is less forcibly engaged, because we can guess, in great measure, how the *dénouement* will be brought about. Yet the subject appears to have been reluctantly dismissed, even in the last and unnecessary scene, where the same mistakes are continued, till they have lost the power of affording any entertainment at all.'

Dr Drake, in defending our author from the indiscriminate censure of Steevens, observes, that 'if we consider the construction of the fable, the narrowness of its basis, and that its powers of entertainment are almost exclusively confined to a continued deception of the external senses, we must confess that Shakespeare has not only improved on the Plautian model, but, making allowance for a somewhat too coarse vein of humor, has given to his production all the interest and variety that the nature and the limits of his subject would permit '

PERSONS REPRESENTED.

SOLINUS, duke of Ephesus.
ÆGEON, a merchant of Syracuse

ANTIPHOLUS of Ephesus, } Twin brothers, and sons to Ægeon and Æmilia, but unknown to each other.
ANTIPHOLUS of Syracuse,

DROMIO of Ephesus, } Twin brothers, and attendants
DROMIO of Syracuse, } on the two Antipholuses
BALTHAZAR, a merchant
ANGELO, a goldsmith
A MERCHANT, creditor to Angelo.
PINCH, a schoolmaster and conjurer.

ÆMILIA, wife to Ægeon, an abbess at Ephesus.
ADRIANA, wife to Antipholus of Ephesus.
LUCIANA, her sister

Luce, her servant
A Courtezan

Jailer, Officers, and other Attendants

Scene, Ephesus

COMPENDIUM OF THE PLAY.

A RICH merchant of Syracuse, named Ægeon, and
a poor man of the same city, became the fathers of
twin sons, each pair exactly resembling each other in
feature the children of the latter are purchased by
the citizen, who bestows them on his sons as attendants Ægeon, with his wife and family, shortly after
visits Epidamnum ; and on their return, the ship in
which they sail is split asunder by a violent storm.
which separates the husband from the wife, and each
of the twin brothers from their respective counterparts
Ægeon, with his younger son and attendant, is rescued
from his perilous condition, and conveyed to Syracuse
Arrived at years of maturity, the young man is anxious
to procure some intelligence of his mother and brother,
and, with the consent of his father. quits his home,
and at length, in company with his servant, arrives
at Ephesus, where the elder Antipholus, who separated from his mother has long resided, in high favor
with the duke, at whose desire he has united himself
to a lady of fortune, who now mistakes the stranger
for her husband, insisting that he shall accompany her
home to dinner : the real husband arrives during the
20

repast, and finds his own doors barred against his entrance The perplexities, arising from the confusion of the masters and their servants, induce the Syracusan youth to suppose himself under the influence of witchcraft, and he takes refuge in a religious house, whither his mother had retired, and had long presided as abbess The Ephesian dame, supposing the refugee to be her husband, complains to the duke of the conduct of the abbess, who refuses to deliver him up to the custody of his wife The simultaneous appearance of the young men and their servants now unravels the mystery In the mean time, Ægeon lands at Ephesus, and is about to lose his head for a violation of the law in entering a hostile city, when he is ransomed by his son, from whom he had parted at Syracuse, and recognizes, in the person of the abbess, his long-lost wife, Æmilia

J O Halliwell says The materials of which the 'Comedy of Errors' is constructed chiefly belong to the cycle of farce, but they have been worked into a comedy by a wonderful effort of dramatic power, the lighter character, however, remaining prominent in particular scenes Comedy would allow the two Antipholuses with a license similar to that which sanctions the resemblance between Sebastian and Viola in 'Twelfth Night,' but the two Dromios, in conjunction with the former, certainly belong to farce. The admirable manner in which the mistakes arising from these identities are conducted, and the dignity given to the whole by the introduction of fine poetry most artistically interwoven, are indicative of that high dramatic genius which belongs almost exclusively to Shakespeare. The poetical conversation between Luciana and Antipholus of Syracuse reminds us forcibly of the 'Son-

nets,' and the similar ideas in the former are strengthened in power by being associated with a dramatic
narrative , for had Shakespeare not been a dramatist,
he would scarcely have ranked as so great a poet   No
play of Shakespeare's, whether either effectively read
or acted, affords as many subjects for broad merriment
as this.

HISTORICAL SUMMARY OF 'MACBETH.'

MALONE has assigned to the year 1606 the composition of this great effort of our author's genius, which has been regarded as the medium of dexterous and graceful flattery to James I, a lineal descendant of Banquo, who is charged by the old historians with a participation in the murder of Duncan, although for very obvious reasons Shakespeare has here represented him as innocent of that cruel deed

The original narrative of these events is contained in the *Scotorum Historiæ* of Hector Boethius, whence it was translated into the Scottish dialect by John Bellenden, and afterwards into English by Holinshed, from whose Chronicles Shakespeare closely followed it The awful incantations and mysterious agency of the witches in this tragedy could not fail to be highly gratifying to the pedantic vanity of a monarch, whose prejudices in favor of the reality of witchcraft or enchantment are well known

'This play,' says Dr Johnson, 'is deservedly celebrated for the propriety of its fictions, and solemnity, grandeur, and variety of its action, but it has no nice discriminations of character the events are too great to admit the influence of particular dispositions ; and the course of the action necessarily determines the conduct of the agents. The danger of ambition is well described, and I know not whether it may not be said, in defence of some parts which now seem improbable,

W. VON KAULBACH, PINX.

SLEEP-WALKING SCENE.

Macbeth, Act V, Scene I.

that in Shakespeare's time it was necessary to warn credulity against vain and illusive predictions The passions are directed to their true end. Lady Macbeth is merely detested , and though the courage of Macbeth preserves some esteem, yet every reader rejoices at his fall '

PERSONS REPRESENTED.

DUNCAN, king of Scotland
MALCOLM, }
DONALBAIN, } his sons.
MACBETH, } generals of the king's army.
BANQUO, }
MACDUFF, }
LENOX, }
ROSSE, }
MENTETH, } noblemen of Scotland
ANGUS, }
CATHNESS, }
FLEANCE, son to Banquo.
SIWARD, earl of Northumberland, general of the English forces
YOUNG SIWARD, his son
SEYTON, an officer attending on Macbeth.
SON TO MACDUFF
AN ENGLISH DOCTOR. A SCOTCH DOCTOR.
A SOLDIER. A PORTER AN OLD MAN.

LADY MACBETH.
LADY MACDUFF.

GENTLEWOMAN attending on Lady Macbeth.
HECATE, and THREE WITCHES

Lords, Gentlemen, Officers, Soldiers, Murderers, Attendants, and Messengers

The Ghost of Banquo, and several other Apparitions

SCENE, in the end of the fourth act, lies in England, through the rest of the play, in Scotland, and, chiefly, at Macbeth's castle

COMPENDIUM OF THE PLAY

DUNCAN, king of Scotland, is rescued from the calamities of foreign invasion and domestic treason by the valor of his generals Macbeth and Banquo, who, after the defeat of the enemy, are returning in triumph, when they are arrested in their progress by three witches, who salute Macbeth by the titles of Cawdor and king, at the same time foretelling that Banquo shall be the father of a race of kings, although he shall never be in possession of the crown. After the announcement of these prophecies, the witches vanish, and messengers arrive from Duncan with the intelligence that the rebellious thane of Cawdor is condemned to death, and that his title is conferred on Macbeth, whose ambition is now panting for the fulfilment of the remainder of the prediction: overcome by the suggestions of his wife, he murders his sovereign in his sleep, during a visit with which he honors him By the artful contrivances of the guilty pair, the king's two sons, Malcolm and Donalbain, are suspected of parricide, and compelled to purchase their safety by flight . The sovereignty now devolves on Macbeth, who, fearful of the prophecy which assigns the crown to the posterity of Banquo, resolves to free himself of his apprehensions by the assassination both of him and his only son the father is slain, but his son Fleance escapes under favor of the night. In the meantime, Malcolm, the eldest son of Duncan, resides in the English court, under the protection of Edward the Confessor, who raises a large army in his behalf, under command of Siward, Earl of Northumberland, which is strengthened by the arrival of Macduff, the thane of Fife, who, in consequence of Macbeth's jealousy, is compelled to quit his country after his departure, the inhuman tyrant wreaks his vengeance on that nobleman's wife and children, all of whom he causes to be murdered The two friends, with their English auxiliaries, now proceed towards Scotland, where they are joined by a number of discontented nobles Macbeth is defeated and slain; his wretched wife, tormented with remorse, puts a period to her existence ; and Malcolm is restored to the throne of his ancestors

Let us give a brief analysis of its principal characters, it may be called a sublime homily on the weakness of human nature—a startling warning, spoken as it were, in words of thunder, and written in characters of blood, against dallying with temptation. Macbeth is gradually led to do that which he persuades himself he cannot avoid—he consents to become a murderer, because he believes that fate has willed it so , he is not the first or the last great criminal who has cast his sins upon a supposed fatal and indisputable ordinance, and who believes, or

professes to believe, that he was predestined to evil.
He is brave and just before he is tempted, but when
tempted strongly, he yields, and falls from the warrior
to the tyrant—timorous, cunning and blood-thirsty.
When he slays the unoffending Duncan he first reasons
strongly against the act, tries to escape from its commission—his conscience wrestles with him, and represents the virtues of the meek king pleading like angels
'against the deep damnation' of the deed, and when
the act is done, it is instantly repented, and the murderer stands aghast at his soul-destroying work.   The
poet has here presented us with an awful picture of
the terrors of conscience—the shuddering murderer
trembling at every sound, and peopling the air with
avenging voices uttering strange and fearful threaten-
ings, but after Macbeth becomes deeply steeped in
blood and familiar with crime, we may observe the
savage premeditation of his murders   When giving
directions for the death of Banquo, he addresses the
assassins thus 'Was it not yesterday we spoke together?' evincing a perfect indifference to the intended destruction of his old associate and fellow-
soldier, he has altogether got rid of the 'compunctious
visitings' which shook him when engaged in the murder
of Duncan   It has been said that a man who commits
one murder, and escapes detection or punishment,
seldom remains single in his crime—he is hounded
on by his impetuous and savage desires again to
imbrue his hands in blood, thus is it with Macbeth
he feels that for him there is no retreat, and he adds
crime to crime, until he becomes a mere vulgar tyrant,
surrounding his nobility with spies, and, in his fear,
devoting to death even the innocent, whom he merely
suspected to be dangerous.

Lady Macbeth is such a character as Shakespeare alone, of all dramatists, could have painted—terrible even to sublimity in her determinate wickedness— fiend-like in the savage obduracy of her nature ; the bitter scoffer of the irresolute pleadings of departing virtue, and the expiring throes of conscience in her guilty partner, still she is never utterly beyond our sympathy She urges her husband to the murder of Duncan, but she bears no hatred to the mild old king he is an obstacle in her path to greatness, and must be removed. When bending over his couch, on the fearful night of his murder, when, amidst the howlings of the storm and the rack of the elements, there were

'Lamentings heard i' the air ; strange screams of death
And prophesying, with accents terrible '—

even then, unmoved by all these horrors, she contemplates his destruction by her own hand, but the resemblance between him and her aged father shoots athwart her mind, and she experiences a momentary tenderness for the unsuspecting and defenceless monarch She is a woman still But this softening of her stern nature is but transient, it does not last long enough to interfere with her dread resolve, she feels, but smothers human sympathies, and brings them into bondage to her adamantine will This fearful woman is a faithful and affectionate wife · we view her with none of the abhorrence which is excited in us towards Regan and Goneril, the cruel and unnatural daughters of the aged Lear, whom, with an exquisite probability, Shakespeare also makes unchaste and treacherous wives When, at the banquet, Macbeth raves about the ghost of Banquo, who glares horribly upon him and points to the

'Twenty trenched gashes on his head,'

she dismisses the guests in confusion, but when they are gone, she utters not one word of reproach, but gently tells him that he lacks rest

She has shown no sign of repentance—spoken no word of compunction, yet we see her punishment is begun, the torture of the mind tells on the fevered frame, the seed which she had sown in blood, though it had grown to be a vigorous plant, had borne no fruit; and when she next comes upon the scene, it is when brokenhearted and dying she utters in her sleep those fearful thoughts which, in her watchful moments, she had kept closed up in her own sad, yet hardened heart

After Macbeth and his ambitious wife, there are few strongly marked characters in the play, except Macduff, thane of Fife, who had fled with Malcolm and Donalbain, and on whom Macbeth wreaks vengeance by destroying his wife and children   Macduff gladly joins Malcolm in his vengeance on Macbeth, and at one point of the play Macduff, in the hands of a good actor, overshadows Macbeth in the grandeur of his declamation for revenge   Duncan is a mild and virtuous sovereign, but he calls for little further comment   the softness of his nature is traceable in the timid characters of his two sons, who, by their disgraceful flight, at first incur the suspicion of being his murderers   Banquo is the opposite of Macbeth, being both a brave and virtuous general   The witches solicit him also during sleep to some horrible act, but he prays against a repetition of the temptation, while Macbeth is on the watch for opportunity

This great tragedy conveys a grand moral precept poetical justice is dealt out rigidly to its chief actors.

Lady Macbeth, as the greatest criminal, is the greatest sufferer: madness, and a supposed suicide, close her career of guilt and gloom; and her husband meets his death by the same violent means as those by which he had attained his regal but wretched eminence, while the punishment of both is brought about by their own evil actions.

Scenes of terror, such as are found in this tragedy, stand alone; otherwise, says Schlegel, 'the tragic muse might exchange her mask for the head of Medusa.'

HISTORICAL SUMMARY OF 'KING JOHN.'

THE materials of the present play are to be found in the Chronicles of Holinshed , Shakespeare, however, has closely followed the incidents of a former drama, entitled 'The troublesome Raigne of John king of England, with the Discoverie of King Richard Cordelion's base Son, vulgarly named the Bastard Faulconbridge , also the Death of King John at Swinstead Abbey : as it was sundry times publikely acted by the Queenes Majesties Players in the honourable Cittie of London ' This piece was printed anonymously in the year 1591 on its republication in 1611, the bookseller, for whom it was printed, fraudulently inserted the letters 'W Sh ' in the title-page , and in a third edition in 1622, the name of ' William Shakespeare' is inserted at full length Pope attributes the composition of this crude performance to the joint pens of Shakespeare and Rowley, though without stating his authority

This tragedy is supposed by Malone to have been written in 1596, though it was not printed till 1623. It is the only one of our poet's uncontested plays that is not entered in the books of the Stationers' Company

'The tragedy of King John,' says Dr Johnson, ' though not written with the utmost power of Shakespeare, is varied with a very pleasing interchange of incidents and characters. The lady's grief is very

W. VON KAULBACH, PINX.

PRINCE ARTHUR AND HUBERT.

King John, Act IV., Scene I.

affecting, and the character of the Bastard contains
that mixture of greatness and levity, which this author
delighted to exhibit '

PERSONS REPRESENTED

KING JOHN
PRINCE HENRY, his son, afterwards King Henry III
ARTHUR, duke of Bretagne, son of Geffrey, late duke
of Bretagne, the elder brother of King John.
WILLIAM MARESHALL, earl of Pembroke
GEFFREY FITZ-PETER, earl of Essex, chief justiciary
of England
WILLIAM LONGSWORD, earl of Salisbury
ROBERT BIGOT, earl of Norfolk.
HUBERT DE BURGH, chamberlain to the king
ROBERT FAULCONBRIDGE, son of Sir Robert Faulcon-
bridge
PHILIP FAULCONBRIDGE, his half-brother, bastard
son to King Richard the First
JAMES GURNEY, servant to Lady Faulconbridge.
PETER OF POMFRET, a prophet.

PHILIP, king of France
LEWIS, the Dauphin
ARCHDUKE OF AUSTRIA
CARDINAL PANDULPH, the pope's legate.
MELUN, a French lord.
CHATILLON, ambassador from France to King John

ELINOR, widow of King Henry II. and mother of
King John

CONSTANCE, mother to Arthur.

BLANCH, daughter to Alphonso, king of Castile, and niece to King John

LADY FAULCONBRIDGE, mother to the Bastard and Robert Faulconbridge.

Lords, Ladies, Citizens of Angiers, Sheriff, Heralds, Officers, Soldiers, Messengers, and other Attendants.

SCENE, sometimes in England, and sometimes in France.

COMPENDIUM OF THE PLAY.

AT the death of Richard Cœur de Lion, the English crown is seized by John from the feeble hands of his nephew Arthur, the rightful heir, whose claims are supported by Philip, king of France   the prospect of uniting the English territories with his own kingdom, by the marriage of the Dauphin with a niece of John, induces the French monarch to withdraw his protection from Arthur, when the arrival of a legate from the Pope prevents the completion of the treaty, and rekindles the flames of war   Philip is defeated in a general engagement; and Arthur, now a captive, is committed by his uncle to the custody of one Hubert, with secret orders to put him to death   Softened by the innocence and entreaties of the youth, Hubert ventures to disobey the cruel

mandate, Arthur loses his life in an endeavor to
effect his escape from the castle in which he is confined, and his lifeless body is discovered by some discontented nobles, who are resolved to emancipate
themselves from the thraldom of the tyrant John by
the desperate measure of inviting the Dauphin to
assume the crown, under the sanction of the papal
court On the arrival of the young prince, John is
compelled to purchase a disgraceful peace by a pusil-
lanimous surrender of his regal dignity into the hands
of the cardinal legate, who now hastens to arrest the
progress of the Dauphin The mediation proves
ineffectual, and hostilities are about to recommence,
when the intelligence of the loss of a large supply
of French troops on the Goodwin Sands, together
with the defection of the English auxiliaries, damps
the ardor of the French prince, and disposes him to
terms of peace In the meantime John is poisoned
by a monk, and is succeeded in his government by his
son, Henry the Third

In considering this play without any reference to
history, we must speak of it very highly, though des-
titute of the poetic halo which beautifies many of the
bard's more imaginative dramas, it is still invested
with a warlike and solemn grandeur We feel that
the theme is kingdoms and the chief actors princes.
The air seems to resound with the brazen clang of
trumpets and the clash of arms, the sunbeams gild
the banners of rival armies, and dance upon the
plumed crests of thousands of brave knights The
secret motives of monarchs are divined with the accuracy of a seer, and the hearts of kings laid bare in
the sight of the people. The interest never flags for
a moment ; the play has several strongly marked char-

acters, most effectively grouped together. The dark portrait of John is finely contrasted with the bold chivalrous bastard, Faulconbridge, 'the very spirit of Plantagenet,' who appears to be entirely a creation of the poet   He is the sunshine of the picture.   His mirthful sallies relieve the oppressed spirits, after some of the painful tragic scenes, and chase away the gloomy shadows which seem rapidly closing around us   His fine natural spirits, shrewd worldly sense, undaunted courage, and witty, sparkling discourse, bespeak him a son of the lion-hearted Richard   The brave, reckless, but manly-tempered hero of Palestine seems to live again in him, somewhat modified by difference of station   Witnessing the interested motives of all around him, he exclaims, 'Gain, be my lord' for I will worship thee ,' but he is an honest soldier, and serves the king with an undeviating integrity that. was worthy of a nobler master   In this character the poet has shown that great talents and energy employed in a bad cause seldom enjoy a lengthened triumph ; but, like an ill-manned vessel on an unexplored sea, drift about in uncertainty and peril   Faulconbridge becomes a serious man, and accumulated disasters wring from his iron nature a prayer to heaven not to tempt him above his power

Lady Constance is an instance of maternal affection and dangerous ambition.   These united feelings prompt her to claim the crown of England for her child, and thus to plunge the kingdom into a fearful war to gratify her feelings, and to advance her son. The title of John was at the least as good as that of Arthur, if not less liable to objection   But in the final anguish of the bereaved mother we forget the ambition of the woman ; the intensity of her grief is

painfully affecting, and few can listen to the passionate
exclamations wrung from her breaking heart, when
Arthur is captured by his uncle John, without a sympathizing tear Her question to the cardinal, whether
she shall know her child in heaven? and her rejoinder
to the expostulation of King Philip—

'Grief fills up the room of my absent child,' etc ,

pierce every bosom, soften every heart The character
of Arthur is made sweetly touching from the helpless-
ness of infancy, and the extreme gentleness of his
nature The poet, in deviating slightly from historic
truth, gained, in this instance, a great dramatic advantage The want of ambition and utter unobtrusiveness
of the young prince endear him to us .

'So I were out of prison and kept sheep,
I should be as merry as the day is long '

That is his modest thought , happy had it been for
him could it have been realized , but the grim red-
handed fiend of murder dogs his guileless steps, and
drives him to a blood-stained grave

There are two scenes which stand prominently out
from the rest the one where the troubled tyrant
works upon Hubert to undertake the death of Arthur,
in which the fiendish character of John is shown without a veil , and the other where Hubert endeavors to
execute his revolting commission of burning out the
eyes of the young prince, but is diverted from his
savage purpose by the poor boy's tears and entreaties
These two scenes deserve to be ranked with the grand-
est tragic efforts of the poet The scene where John
recriminates the guilt of Arthur's death upon Hubert
21

and equivocates respecting the warrant for it, is also highly Shakespearian

The closing scene is touched by a master hand ; we pity the death-struck wretch writhing in anguish before us, who is described as singing in his agony. Painful is his reply to his son's inquiry as to his state, solemnly affecting from its profound and irredeemable misery :

> ' Poisoned : ill fare ! dead, forsook, cast off ! '

A terrible retribution has come upon the tyrant ; body and soul seem perishing before us.

MR. MACREADY AS RICHARD II.

King Richard II., Act V., Scene V.

HISTORICAL SUMMARY OF 'KING RICHARD II'

THIS play comprises little more than the last two years of the reign of Richard II. The action of the drama commences with Bolingbroke's challenge to Mowbray, duke of Norfolk, on an accusation of high treason, which took place in 1398, and it concludes with the murder of King Richard at Pomfret castle towards the end of 1400, or the beginning of the following year. Holinshed furnished the facts which the poet dramatized: the speech of the bishop of Carlisle in favor of Richard's divine right, and exemption from human jurisdiction, is copied, almost *verbatim*, from that old historian

The year 1593 is the date assigned by Malone to the production of this drama, which was printed four times during the lifetime of our author, the first two editions appearing in 1597 and 1598, without the scene of the deposition, which was first appended in 1608. The next impression was that of 1615.

PERSONS REPRESENTED.

KING RICHARD THE SECOND
EDMUND OF LANGLEY, duke of York, } uncles to the
JOHN OF GAUNT, duke of Lancaster, } king

HENRY, surnamed Bolingbroke, duke of Hereford, son
    to John of Gaunt, afterwards King Henry IV.
DUKE OF AUMERLE, son to the duke of York.
MOWBRAY, duke of Norfolk.
DUKE OF SURREY
EARL OF SALISBURY
EARL BERKLEY
BUSHY,
BAGOT, } creatures to King Richard.
GREEN,
EARL OF NORTHUMBERLAND
HENRY PERCY, his son
LORD ROSS   LORD WILLOUGHBY   LORD FITZWATER.
BISHOP OF CARLISLE.   ABBOT OF WESTMINSTER.
LORD MARSHAL, and another Lord
SIR PIERCE OF EXTON   SIR STEPHEN SCROOP.
Captain of a band of Welshmen.

QUEEN to King Richard.
DUCHESS OF GLOSTER
DUCHESS OF YORK.
Lady attending on the Queen

Lords, Heralds, Officers, Soldiers, two Gardeners,
    Keeper, Messenger, Groom, and other Attendants

    SCENE, dispersedly in England and Wales.

COMPENDIUM OF THE PLAY.

    HENRY BOLINGBROKE, eldest son of John of Gaunt,
duke of Lancaster, accuses Mowbray, duke of Nor-

folk, of high treason, and, in confirmation of his
assertion, challenges him to single combat, which is
eagerly accepted by his opponent. At the appointed
time, the combatants enter the lists, and the conflict
is about to commence, when the king interposes, and
pronounces a sentence of perpetual banishment on
Norfolk, while the exile of Bolingbroke is limited to
the period of six years   Shortly after the departure
of his son, John of Gaunt dies, and his property and
estates are unjustly seized by the indigent monarch
Stung by this scandalous act of oppression, Bolingbroke takes advantage of the king's absence in Ireland, and arrives in England, where, by his artful
professions of loyalty, together with solemn protesta-
tions of circumscribing his views within the reasonable demand of a repeal of his exile and a recovery
of his patrimony, he insensibly acquires a power too
formidable to be resisted ; and the unfortunate Richard
is compelled to resign his crown into the hands of his
cousin , after which he is confined in Pomfret castle,
where he is put to death by the connivance of Bolingbroke

Between the death of John and the commencement
of this play four kings had successively worn the crown
of England, and a period of nearly two centuries had
elapsed ; but this and the seven plays which follow are
one continuous history   A certain connection is kept
up between them, and they may be termed one perfect
historical romance, of which the different plays con-
stitute the books, and the acts and scenes the chap-
ters   Disagreeing with Schlegel as to the invariable
historical fidelity of these productions, and condemn-
ing the adulatory spirit and eager 'hero-worship'
which would call that history which the poet only

intended as a romance, I still gladly avail myself of
the happily expressed thought of the great German
critic, and say that this series of dramas 'furnishes
examples of the political course of the world, applica-
ble to all times.' *This mirror of kings should be the
manual of young princes;* from it they may learn the
intrinsic dignity of their hereditary vocation, but they
will also learn from it the difficulties of their situation,
the dangers of usurpation, the inevitable fall of tyranny, which buries itself under its attempts to obtain
a firmer foundation, lastly, the ruinous consequences
of the weaknesses, errors, and crimes of kings, for
whole nations and many subsequent generations

These historic dramas must be regarded as lofty
fictions, fictions teaching truth, great political para-
bles based on facts, but rearing their high and graceful
pinnacles into the realms of imagination But if they
are pronounced to be strict literal history, then must
we say that much of history is merely what Napo-
leon declared it to be—'a fiction agreed upon '

Schlegel says '' In ' King Richard the Second ' the
poet exhibits to us a noble kingly nature, at first obscured by levity and the errors of unbridled youth,
and afterwards purified by misfortune, and rendered
more highly splendid and illustrious When he has
lost the love and reverence of his subjects, and is on
the point of losing also his throne, he then feels with
painful inspiration the elevated vocation of the kingly
dignity and its prerogatives over personal merit and
changeable institutions When the earthly crown has
fallen from off his head he first appears as a king
whose innate nobility no humiliation can annihilate
This is felt by a poor groom he is shocked that his
master's favorite horse should have carried the proud

Bolingbroke at his coronation ; he visits the captive king in his prison and shames the desertion of the great. The political history of the deposition is represented with extraordinary knowledge of the world— the ebb of fortune on the one hand and the swelling tide on the other, which carries everything along with it ; while Bolingbroke acts as a king, and his adherents behave towards him as if he really were so, he still continues to give out that he comes with an armed band merely for the sake of demanding his birthright and the removal of abuses   The usurpation has been long completed before the word is pronounced and the thing publicly avowed.   John of Gaunt is a model of chivalrous truth   he stands there like a pillar of the olden time which he had outlived

HISTORICAL SUMMARY OF 'KING HENRY IV.'—PART I

———

THIS drama was first entered at Stationer's Hall February 25, 1597-8 its production is assigned by Malone to the year 1597, while Mr Chalmers and Dr. Drake suppose it to have been written during the preceding year. No fewer than five quarto editions of this play were published during the lifetime of our author, in 1598, 1599, 1604, 1608 and 1613.

The action of the First Part of Henry the Fourth begins immediately after the defeat of the Scots at Holmedon in 1402, and terminates with the defeat and death of Hotspur at Shrewsbury about ten months afterwards

Dr Johnson observes, that ' Shakespeare has apparently designed a regular connection of these dramatic histories from Richard the Second to Henry the Fifth. King Henry, at the end of Richard the Second, declares his purpose to visit the Holy Land, which he resumes in the first speech of this play The complaint made by King Henry, in the last act of Richard the Second, of the wildness of his son, prepares the reader for the frolics which are here to be recounted, and the characters which are now to be exhibited '

It may be remarked, however, that the introduction of the prince at this early period of history is to be attributed solely to the desire of the poet to produce dramatic effect ; since, at the time when the conspiracy

FROM A PHOTOGRAPH BY N. SARONY.

CHARLES FISHER AS FALSTAFF.

First Part of King Henry IV, Act II, Scene IV.

of the duke of Aumerle was discovered, Prince Henry
was but twelve years old , and, therefore, too young as
yet to be a partaker in the debaucheries of London
taverns   It is also extremely probable, that the licen-
tious habits, attributed to him by the English chroni-
clers of the sixteenth century, have been greatly exag-
gerated.

PERSONS REPRESENTED

KING HENRY THE FOURTH
HENRY, prince of Wales, } sons to the king
PRINCE JOHN OF LANCASTER,
EARL OF WESTMORELAND, } friends to the king
SIR WALTER BLUNT,
THOMAS PERCY, earl of Worcester
HENRY PERCY, earl of Northumberland
HENRY PERCY, surnamed Hotspur, his son
EDMUND MORTIMER, earl of March
SCROOP, archbishop of York
ARCHIBALD, earl of Douglas
OWEN GLENDOWER
SIR RICHARD VERNON
SIR JOHN FALSTAFF
SIR MICHAEL, a friend of the archbishop of York.
POINS
GADSHILL
PETO.
BARDOLPH.

LADY PERCY, wife to Hotspur, and sister to Mortimer

LADY MORTIMER, daughter to Glendower, and wife to Mortimer.

MRS QUICKLY, hostess of a tavern in Eastcheap.

Lords, Officers, Sheriff, Vintner, Chamberlain, Drawers, two Carriers, Travellers and Attendants.

SCENE, England

COMPENDIUM OF THE PLAY.

THE chief characters in this play are Falstaff, Prince Henry, Percy and King Henry. After the deposition and death of the unfortunate Richard, the attention of King Henry is directed to the incursions of the Scots, who, under conduct of Douglas, advance to the borders of England, where they are totally routed by the celebrated Percy, surnamed Hotspur The intelligence of this victory no sooner reaches the ears of the king, than, regardless of the debt of gratitude due to the powerful family of the Percies, he demands the prisoners taken in the late struggle, among whom was the renowned Douglas , contrary to the practice of those times, when the custody and destination of captives were determined at the discretion of the conquering general. Exasperated at this unexpected mandate, Hotspur dismisses all his prisoners without ransom, and with his relatives and dependents raises the standard of revolt against the sovereign, whose elevation they had so recently effected Having formed a treaty of alliance with the Scottish and Welsh leaders,

the insurgents arrive at Shrewsbury, where they are
encountered by the king in person   A decisive battle
ensues, in which Hotspur is slain, and the rebels
sustain a signal defeat   The only two lady characters
are Ladies Percy and Mortimer, the former a very
pretty character.   The remainder of this drama is occupied with the amusing detail of the frolics of the
Prince of Wales and his merry companions, among
whom Sir John Falstaff occupies the most conspicuous
part   The meeting of Sir John, Poins and Prince Hal
and their pranks at the Boar's Head Tavern in Eastcheap, and elsewhere with their attendants, Bardolph,
Peto and Mrs. Quickly, hostess of the tavern, and
their superb fooling of Sir John in the robbery at
Gad's Hill, form one the of most jovial series of pictures ever presented in literature

The transactions contained in the 'First Part of
King Henry IV.' are comprised within the period of
about ten months ; for the action commences with the
news brought of Hotspur having defeated the Scots
under Archibald Earl of Douglas, at Holmedon (or
Halidown Hall), which battle was fought on Holy-
rood day (the 14th of September), 1402 , and it closes
with the battle of Shrewsbury on Saturday, the 21st
of July, 1403

HISTORICAL SUMMARY OF 'KING HENRY IV '—PART II

THE composition of this play has been assigned by Malone to the year 1599, while Mr Chalmers and Dr Drake suppose it to have been written as early as 1596 or 1597   The play of 'Henry IV' is mentioned in the list of Shakespeare's works, in Meres' 'Wits' Treasury,' 1598 , and, by the Epilogue to this drama, it appears to have preceded 'King Henry V ,' which is fixed with some accuracy to 1599   It was entered at Stationers' Hall, August 23d, 1600, and the first two editions of it in quarto were published in the same year   Its action comprehends a period of nine years, commencing with Hotspur's death in 1403, and terminating with the coronation of King Henry V. in 1412–13   'These two plays,' says Dr Johnson, 'will appear to every reader, who shall peruse them without ambition of critical discoveries, to be so connected, that the second is merely a sequel to the first , to be two only because they are too long to be one '

In reading Holinshed for these plays, our poet's eye was evidently eager in quest of scattered hints of personal character, and on these, whenever he was fortunate enough to meet with them, his exuberant imagination worked with boldness.   The dismissal of Falstaff, as one of Henry's dissolute companions, is conformable to the old historian, but his committal to the

FALSTAFF AND HIS PAGE.

Second Part of King Henry IV. Act I, Scene II.

Fleet is an act of severity volunteered by Shakespeare.
A reference to Stowe in this case would have been
eminently useful to him   the prince's companions are
there disposed of in a manner gratifying to the feelings
of humanity and consistent with the claims of justice
'After his coronation, King Henry called unto him
all those young lords and gentlemen who were the
followers of his young acts, to every one of whom he
gave rich gifts , and then commanded, that as many as
would change their manners, as he intended to do,
should abide with him in his court , and to all that
would persevere in their former like conversation, he
gave express commandment, upon pain of their heads,
never after that day to come in his presence '

'None of Shakespeare's plays,' adds Dr Johnson,
'are more read than the First and Second Parts of
Henry the Fourth   perhaps no author has ever in
two plays afforded so much delight   The great events
are interesting, for the fate of kingdoms depends on
them , the slighter occurrences are diverting, and,
except one or two, sufficiently probable , the incidents
are multiplied with wonderful fertility of invention ;
and the characters diversified with the utmost nicety
of discernment, and the profoundest skill in the nature
of man

'The prince, who is the hero both of the comic and
tragic part, is a young man of great abilities and violent passions , whose sentiments are right, though his
actions are wrong, whose virtues are obscured by
negligence, and whose understanding is dissipated by
levity   In his idle hours he is rather loose than
vicious, but when the responsibility of succession to
the crown comes in his turn he proves himself a true
king '

PERSONS REPRESENTED.

KING HENRY THE FOURTH.
HENRY, prince of Wales, afterwards King
    Henry V.,
THOMAS, duke of Clarence,
PRINCE JOHN OF LANCASTER, afterwards } his sons.
    (2 Henry V.) duke of Bedford,
PRINCE HUMPHREY OF GLOSTER, after-
    wards (2 Henry V.) duke of Gloster,

EARL OF WARWICK;
EARL OF WESTMORELAND, } of the king's party.
GOWER, HARCOURT,
LORD CHIEF JUSTICE of the King's Bench.
A GENTLEMAN attending on the Chief Justice.
EARL OF NORTHUMBERLAND,
SCROOP, archbishop of York, } enemies
LORD MOWBRAY, LORD HASTINGS, } to the king.
LORD BARDOLPH, SIR JOHN COLEVILLE,
TRAVERS and MORTON, domestics of Northumberland.
FALSTAFF, BARDOLPH, PISTOL, and PAGE.
POINS and PETO, attendants on Prince Henry.
SHALLOW and SILENCE, country justices.
DAVY, servant to Shallow.
MOULDY, SHADOW, WART, FEEBLE, and BULLCALF,
    recruits.
FANG and SNARE, sheriff's officers.
RUMOR.   A PORTER.
A DANCER, speaker of the Epilogue.

LADY NORTHUMBERLAND.
LADY PERCY.

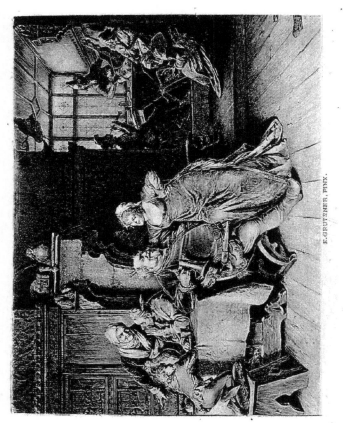

FALSTAFF AND DOLL TEARSHEET.

E. GRUTZNER, PINX.

Second Part of King Henry IV., Act II., Scene IV.

Hostess Quickly.
Doll Tear-sheet.

Lords and other Attendants; Officers, Soldiers, Messenger, Drawers, Beadles, Grooms, etc.

Scene, England.

COMPENDIUM OF THE PLAY

After the defeat and death of Hotspur at Shrewsbury, the king despatches his son Prince John of Lancaster and the earl of Westmoreland, at the head of a large army, to encounter the northern insurgents, under the command of Scroop, archbishop of York. The two armies meet at Gaultree Forest in Yorkshire, where Prince John, unwilling to hazard a general engagement, invites the discontented chieftains to a conference, with whom he concludes a treaty, promising a full redress of their alleged grievances, and stipulating for a dismissal of the troops on either side   The royalist forces however receive secret instructions, and, by an unparalleled act of perfidy, are commanded to destroy the disbanded insurgents, while the archbishop and his coadjutors are led to immediate execution   In the meantime, Prince Henry is summoned from the society of his dissipated companions to attend the death-bed of his father, whom he finds in a swoon, with the crown on his pillow   Judging him to have breathed his last, the prince removes the diadem —an act which incurs the bitter reproaches of the king when he awakes his son justifies his conduct to the satisfaction of the dying monarch ; and no sooner assumes the regal dignity, than he dismisses forever from his presence Sir John Falstaff and the companions of his youthful excesses, and resolves to signalize his reign by the splendor of his achievements and the virtues of his character The success of Falstaff at the Battle of Shrewsbury set up the old knight in every way—in purse, in character and influence The revels are continued and some new characters introduced Doll Tear-sheet, Davy, Shallow's servant, and the scene of the recruits besides other mirthful scenes at the Boar's Head in Eastcheap

J W Singer says The historical dramas of Shakespeare have become the popular history Vain attempts have been made by Walpole to vindicate the character of King Richard III , and in later times by Mr Luders, to prove that the youthful dissipation ascribed to King Henry V is without foundation The arguments are probable and ingeniously urged, but we still cling to our early notions of 'that mad chap—that same sword and buckler, Prince of Wales.' No plays were ever more read, nor does the inimitable, all powerful genius of the poet ever shine out more than in the two parts of King Henry IV., which may be considered as one long drama divided.

It has been said that 'Falstaff is the summit of Shakespeare's comic invention,' and we may consequently add the most inimitable comic character ever delineated , for who could invent like Shakespeare? Falstaff is now to us hardly a creature of the imagination. He is so definitely and distinctly drawn that the mere reader of these dramas has the complete impression of a personal acquaintance He is surrounded by a group of comic personages from time to time, each of which would have been sufficient to throw any ordinary creation into the shade, but they only serve to make the super-eminent humor of the knight doubly conspicuous What can come nigher to truth and real individual nature than those admirable delineations, Shallow and Silence? How irresistibly comic are all the scenes in which Falstaff is made to humor the fatuity and vanity of this precious pair !

The historic characters are delineated with a felicity and individuality not inferior in any respect Harry Percy is a creation of the first order , and our favorite hare-brained Prince of Wales, in whom mirthful pleasantry and midnight dissipation are mixed up with heroic dignity and generous feeling, is a rival worthy of him. Owen Glendower is another personification, managed with the most consummate skill , and the graver characters are sustained and opposed to each other in a manner peculiar to our great poet.

22

HISTORICAL SUMMARY OF 'KING HENRY V'

FROM a passage in the chorus at the commencement of the fifth act, this drama appears to have been written during the absence of the earl of Essex in Ireland, between April and September, 1599, those being the dates of that nobleman's departure and return   It was entered at Stationers' Hall August 14, 1600, and three editions were published before the death of our author , namely, in 1600, 1602, and 1608   In all of these he choruses are omitted, and the play commences with the fourth speech of the second scene   The historical transactions occupy little more than the first six years of the reign of the illustrious monarch whose exploits are here commemorated, the materials of which have been derived from the Chronicles of Holinshed, and an older play, entitled 'The famous Victories of Henry the Fift, containing the honorable Battle of Agincourt,' which was entered at Stationers' Hall, May 2, 1594

'This play,' says Dr Johnson, 'has many scenes of high dignity, and many of easy merriment   The character of the king is well supported, except in his courtship, where he has neither the vivacity of Hal nor the grandeur of Henry   The humor of Pistol is very happily continued · his character has perhaps been the model of all the bullies that have yet appeared on the English stage   The lines given to the

F. PECHT, PINX.

KING HENRY. KATHARINE. ETC.

King Henry V. Act V. Scene II.

Chorus have many admirers, but the truth is, that in them a little may be praised, and much must be forgiven : nor can it be easily discovered why the intelligence given by the Chorus is more necessary in this play than in many others where it is omitted   The great defect of this play is the emptiness and narrowness of the last act, which a very little diligence might have easily avoided '

PERSONS REPRESENTED.

KING HENRY THE FIFTH.
DUKE OF GLOSTER, }
DUKE OF BEDFORD, } brothers to the king
DUKE OF EXETER, uncle to the king.
DUKE OF YORK, cousin to the king.
EARLS OF SALISBURY, WESTMORELAND, and WARWICK.
ARCHBISHOP OF CANTERBURY.
BISHOP OF ELY. '
EARL OF CAMBRIDGE, }
LORD SCROOP, } conspirators against the king
SIR THOMAS GREY, }
SIR THOMAS ERPINGHAM, GOWER, FLUELLEN, MACMORRIS, JAMY, officers in King Henry's army.
BATES, COURT, WILLIAMS, soldiers in the same.
NYM, BARDOLPH, PISTOL, formerly servants to Falstaff, now soldiers in the same.
BOY, servant to them.   A HERALD.   CHORUS.
CHARLES THE SIXTH, king of France.

LEWIS, the Dauphin
DUKES OF BURGUNDY, ORLEANS, and BOURBON
THE CONSTABLE OF FRANCE
RAMBURES and GRANDPREE, French lords
GOVERNOR OF HARFLEUR
MONTJOY, a French herald
AMBASSADORS to the king of England

ISABEL, queen of France
KATHARINE, daughter of Charles and Isabel
ALICE, a lady attending on the princess Katharine
QUICKLY, Pistol's wife, an hostess

Lords, Ladies Officers, French and English Soldiers,
Messengers, and Attendants

The SCENE, at the beginning of the play, lies in Eng
land, but afterwards, wholly in France

COMPENDIUM OF THE PLAY.

HENRY is no sooner in possession of the English
crown, than he prepares to fulfil the injunctions of his
dying father, and to efface from the minds of his subjects the defects in his title by the splendor of foreign
conquest, in pursuance of which design he now re-
vives an antiquated claim to the sceptre of France,
which he prepares to advocate by assembling a powerful
army. The French court, intimidated at these dem-
onstrations of hostility, basely endeavor to procure the

assassination of the English monarch by profusely
bribing three powerful noblemen, Cambridge, Scroop
and Grey. The conspiracy is brought to light and
punished, and Henry safely arrives in France, and
takes the town of Harfleur by capitulation Sickness
and want of provisions at length diminish his army,
and compel him to retreat in the face of an enemy
five times his superior in numbers, who force him to
risk a general engagement near the village of Agincourt, where he obtains a complete victory, which renders further resistance unavailing The French king
is now reduced to the necessity of submitting to the
hard terms imposed on him by his conqueror, who is
publicly recognized as heir to the crown and united in
marriage to the princess Katharine.

The poet has carefully elaborated the character
of Henry, he introduces him into three dramas, carries him uncontaminated through scenes of riot and
dissipation, represents him repenting his lost hours
with tears of shame and affection, at the feet of his
father, and, on his accession to the "golden rigol, '
after winning the good graces of prelates, nobility, and
people, and passing undaunted through a fearful
ordeal, such as would have overwhelmed many a stout
heart, leaves him on a summit of military glory more
brilliant than had been achieved even by his brave and
illustrious ancestors The fine description by the
Archbishop of Canterbury of the King's reformation,
and the sudden blaze of those virtues and accomplishments which he was not suspected to have possessed, has been aptly applied to Shakespeare himself. Like Henry, the wildness of his youth promised
not the brilliant performances of his manhood. With
the poet, as with the prince,

> 'Consideration like an angel came,
> And whipp'd the offending Adam out of him;
> Leaving his body as a paradise,
> To envelop and contain celestial spirits'

The introductory dialogue between the two bishops, independent of its exquisite beauty, easily and naturally prepares us for the change of the frolicsome idle prince to the serious and majestic king

As a monarch he is drawn with great spirit and power, he is sincere, magnanimous, eloquent, and pious, though it must be confessed his piety is often of a very convenient character   His address to his army before the walls of Harfleur is a model of military oratory, full of manly fire and enthusiasm.   We can fancy the soldiers listening with set teeth, dilated nostrils, and flashing eyes, and then again following him with resistless fury to the breach in the walls of the besieged city   In his warning to the governor of Harfleur is contained the most terribly eloquent description of war in the English language

The mirthful and early pranks of Henry are not forgotten in this play , his acceptance of the glove of the soldier as a challenge, and bestowal of it upon Fluellen, show that his sportive disposition is not extinguished, but tempered by rank and responsibility of station. Still he turns moralist in his extremity, and exclaims to his brother

> 'There is some soul of goodness in things evil,
> Would men observingly distil it out'

Henry's claim upon France was politic but ungenerous, for that unhappy country was distracted by internal broils, possessed a lunatic for a king, and was laid waste by the furious contentions of its own nobles. So far from his having any title to the crown of France, his right to the sovereignty of his own country would not bear examination, and it was to evade inquiry, and that his nobility might not have leisure to conspire against him in England, that he led them to war against France, and the archbishop encourages and justifies the design, that Henry may not pry too closely into the vast possessions of the church Such are the secret springs of war and conquest

In many of his historical plays, but chiefly in this, does Shakespeare evince a patriotic love of his native country, his language is well calculated to excite a natural pride in English bosoms, and we share the enthusiasm with which he paints the hardihood and prowess of his countrymen, but when we reflect upon the past conflicts with France, we should remember that an insular position is exceedingly advantageous England, when governed by a powerful military king, always took advantage of any calamity in France, to make invasions which its temporary weakness and the sea prevented it from readily returning The different occupations of the two armies and their leaders on the eve of battle are pointed out in a manner from which the poet intended us to infer the opposite character of the two nations The French nobility are engaged in frivolous conversation respecting their horses and their armor, and in playing at dice for the prisoners whom they assume they shall capture the next day The English are occupied in patient watching and serious meditation upon the fearfully unequal contest in which a few hours will involve them. This comparison is hardly just, but a little exultation was both natural and pardonable in a poet living at a period not more distant from the event than was the reign of Elizabeth.

In this play we hear the last of Falstaff, his death is related by Mrs Quickly We cannot help feeling sad for the poor old knight, dying in an inn, surrounded only by rude dependents, and the faithful hostess, whom we respect for her kind attachment to him to the last.   No wife or child is near , no gentle kindred hand to do kind offices in the hour of weakness and despondency   In his half-delirious moments his last joke was made upon the flea on Bardolph's nose, which he said 'was a black soul burning in hell-fire.'   The scene between the Welsh, Irish, and Scotch captains, each speaking in his peculiar *patois*, is very humorous, but these three do not amount to one Falstaff   The episode between Pistol and the French soldier, whom, by his fierce looks, he frightens into paying a good ransom for his life, is much richer , but the crown of mirth in this play is where the Welshman cudgels Pistol, and makes him eat his leek for having mocked him respecting it.   All the group that surrounded Falstaff are here disposed of , Bardolph and Nym are hanged, the boy is killed by the flying French soldiers after the battle, Mrs. Quickly dies in the hospital, and Pistol sneaks home in disgrace and obscurity

Although there is tragic matter enough in this play, it ends like a comedy—with a marriage of convenience. Henry espoused the princess Katharine on the 2d of June, 1418, in the church of St. John at Troyes   The next day, after he had given a splendid banquet, it was proposed by the French that the event should be honored by a series of tournaments and public rejoicings.   This Henry would not sanction   'I pray,' said he to the French monarch, 'my lord the king to permit, and I command his servants and mine to be all ready to-morrow morning to go and lay siege to Sens, wherein are our enemies   there every man may have jousting and tourneying enough, and may *give proof of his prowess, for there is no finer prowess than that of doing justice on the wicked, in order that the poor people may breathe and live* ' In the exhibition of this courage, activity, and feeling for the lower orders, lay the secret of Henry's popularity He lived four years after his marriage, a period which Shakespeare has left unrecorded , but the death of this heroic king was a scene for the poet   Still only in his thirty-fourth year, a conqueror in the full blaze of military glory, a king beloved by his people almost to idolatry, the husband of a young, beautiful, and accomplished wife, and the father of an infant son, this world was to him a demi-paradise, an earthly Eden , still he breathed his last without one complaint, and was himself calm and resigned, though all around wept as they promised to protect his wife and child The solemn pomp displayed at his funeral was extraordinary ; no such procession had hitherto attended the remains of any English king   His funeral car was preceded and flanked by a crowd of heralds, banner-bearers, and it was followed by some hundreds of knights and esquires in black armor and plumes ; while, far in the rear, travelled the young widow, with a gorgeous and numerous retinue. She, however, does not appear to have been inconsolable, for she was married again shortly after Henry's death to a Welsh gentleman, Sir Owen Tudor, one of the handsomest men of his time   She brought him two sons, of whom the eldest, Edmund, was created earl of Richmond, and his son afterwards ascended the English throne, under the title of Henry the Seventh.

HISTORICAL SUMMARY OF 'KING HENRY VI '—PART I

THIS piece is supposed by Malone to have made its appearance on the stage about the year 1588, and to have been formerly known by the appellation of 'The Historical Play of King Henry VI' The learned commentator has endeavored to prove that it was written neither by Shakespeare nor by the author of the other two plays detailing the events of a subsequent period of the same reign , and these conjectures are confirmed by the manuscript accounts of Henslowe, proprietor of the Rose Tavern, Bankside, which have been since discovered at Dulwich College The entry is dated the 3d of March, 1591 , and the play being the property of Lord Strange's company, and performed at the Rose Theatre, with neither of which Shakespeare had at any time the smallest connection, the testimony of Malone's position as to the antiquity, priority, and insulated origin of this drama, is much corroborated

At this distance of time it is impossible to ascertain on what principle our author's friends, Heminge and Condell, admitted The First Part of 'King Henry VI ' into their volume Malone remarks, that they may have given it a place as a necessary introduction to the two other parts, and because Shakespeare had made some slight alterations, and written a few lines in it.

F. PECHT. PINX.

JOAN OF ARC, THE DAUPHIN, ETC.

First Part of King Henry VI, Act I., Scene II.

The events contained in this dramatic history commence with the funeral of Henry V in 1422, and concluded with the earl of Suffolk being sent to France for Margaret of Anjou, at the close of 1443. The author, however, has not been very precise as to the date and disposition of his facts, since Lord Talbot is killed at the end of the fourth act of this play, who did not really fall till July 13, 1453

PERSONS REPRESENTED.

KING HENRY THE SIXTH
DUKE OF GLOSTER, uncle to the king, and protector
DUKE OF BEDFORD, uncle to the king, and regent of France
THOMAS BEAUFORT, duke of Exeter, great uncle to the king
HENRY BEAUFORT, great uncle to the king, bishop of Winchester, and afterwards cardinal.
JOHN BEAUFORT, earl of Somerset, afterwards duke
RICHARD PLANTAGENET, eldest son of Richard, late earl of Cambridge, afterwards duke of York
EARL OF WARWICK   EARL OF SALISBURY   EARL OF SUFFOLK
LORD TALBOT, afterwards earl of Shrewsbury.
JOHN TALBOT, his son
EDMUND MORTIMER, earl of March
MORTIMER'S KEEPER, and a LAWYER
SIR JOHN FASTOLFE   SIR WILLIAM LUCY
SIR WILLIAM GLANSDALE   SIR THOMAS GARGRAVE.

MAYOR OF LONDON   WOODVILLE, lieutenant of the
    Tower
VERNON, of the white rose, or York faction
BASSET, of the red rose, or Lancaster faction
CHARLES, Dauphin, and afterwards king of France
REIGNIER, duke of Anjou, and titular king of Naples
DUKE OF BURGUNDY   DUKE OF ALENÇON
GOVERNOR OF PARIS   BASTARD OF ORLEANS.
MASTER GUNNER OF ORLEANS, and his SON
GENERAL of the French forces in Bourdeaux
A FRENCH SERGEANT.   A PORTER
AN OLD SHEPHERD, father to Joan la Pucelle

MARGARET, daughter to Reignier, afterwards mar-
    ried to King Henry
COUNTESS OF AUVERGNE
JOAN LA PUCELLE, commonly called Joan of Arc

Fiends appearing to La Pucelle, Lords, Warders of
    the Tower, Heralds, Officers, Soldiers, Messengers
    and several Attendants both on the English and
    French

    SCENE, partly in England, and partly in France.

COMPENDIUM OF THE PLAY

THE sceptre is no sooner transferred from the hands
of the conqueror of France to the feeble grasp of his
son, then an infant, than the favorable opportunity is
seized by the French, who are enabled, by the courage
and energy of a young woman named Joan of Arc, to

recover their former possessions, and to swear allegiance to their native monarch   In the meantime the violent feuds of the dukes of York and Somerset, whose parties are distinguished by white and red roses, lay the foundation of that civil war which was ere long to deluge the whole kingdom with blood   The brave Talbot and his son, together with a small band of faithful followers, are overpowered at Bourdeaux by the united forces of the enemy, and sacrificed to the private jealousy of these hostile nobles, who neglect to send him the necessary reinforcements   The intrepid Joan is at length taken prisoner by the duke of York, and cruelly condemned to the stake, while King Henry is induced, by the artful suggestions of the earl of Suffolk, to solicit the hand of Margaret, daughter of the duke of Anjou   a treaty of alliance is speedily concluded with the father, and the earl despatched to accompany the princess to England.

The earlier scenes of this drama are most artistically adapted to introduce the misrule and dark and bloody struggles of the turbulent reign of Henry   The iron-hand of the hero of Agincourt being laid in the grave, and the enthusiastic patriotism, which was warmed into active existence by his gorgeous and triumphant career, having subsided into the calm stream of common life, the elements of discord break forth.   The fierce contentions of Beaufort and Gloucester show the disordered state of the kingdom consequent upon the supremacy of a child, and are a natural prelude to the savage contests which afterwards took place under the name of the Wars of the Roses

Talbot is a boldly drawn character, he resembles a grim armed giant, whose presence everywhere causes terror and flight, yet he is thoroughly English in his

nature—that is, he possesses all those qualities which
were prominent in the most just and patriotic warriors
of his country in the fifteenth century   Terrible to
his enemies, fierce and savage in war, he is yet mild
and genial to his associates, while on his tenderness as
a father the great interest of his character depends
The scene between him and the Countess of Auvergne
is an admirable episode, full of life and vigor, and written by the pen of genius; if, according to the conjecture of Mr Malone, either Greene or Peele was the
author of this play, it is to be regretted that they have
not left more such scenes for the admiration of posterity   The generosity of Talbot to the crafty but
outwitted Frenchwoman is the result of a noble spirit,
a meaner general would probably have razed her
castle to its foundations, or left it in flames, as a
punishment for her perfidious abuse of the sacred laws
of hospitality

The brave Talbot is at last sacrificed through the
dissensions and treachery of York and Somerset : each
blames the other for neglect, but stands aloof himself;
the intrepid general is surrounded without the walls
of Bordeaux by forces immeasurably superior to his
own, and, after performing prodigies of valor, is slain
Just before his death he has an interview with his son,
whom after an absence of seven years he had sent for,
to tutor in the strategies of war   The meeting is a
melancholy one; certain death awaits them both,
unless avoided by flight—the elder Talbot, grown gray
in peril and in honor, counsels his son to escape, but
will himself remain to meet his fate, the young hero
will not stir from the side of his father, who eventually
dies with the dead body of his son in his arms

In the scene in the Temple Garden, the great Earl

of Warwick is introduced—that Warwick whose after achievements gained for him the title of the ' King-maker,' and although he does not appear so prominently in this play, as in the two following ones, yet here we have the germs of his future character, and a very spirited and Shakespearian speech is uttered by him.   Somerset and Plantagenet having disputed on some legal question, appeal to the earl, who at first declines to side with either party, exclaiming—

> Between two hawks, which flies the higher pitch,
> Between two dogs, which hath the deeper mouth,
> Between two blades, which bears the better temper,
> Between two horses, which doth bear him best,
> Between two girls, which hath the merriest eye,
> I have, perhaps, some shallow spirit of judgment:
> But in these nice sharp quillets of the law,
> Good faith, I am no wiser than a daw.

Something of the princely and chivalrous earl, whose hospitality was as royal and boundless as his wealth, and who kept so many retainers, that sometimes six oxen were eaten by them at a breakfast, is shadowed forth in this hearty and bounding speech   They who are conversant with the language of our poet will need no argument to induce them to believe that it was the work of his pen   In this scene we have detailed the supposed origin of the two badges, the white rose and the red, afterwards worn by the rival houses of York and Lancaster.

The character of Joan la Pucelle, though it has not the finish of Shakespeare's later works, yet partakes of their strength.   It is only to be regretted that he has attributed to satanic agency what was doubtless the result of pure patriotism and vivid religious

enthusiasm ; but the era of the poet was one of intense
and obstinate superstition, when to express a disbelief
in witchcraft was frequently deemed an act of impiety,
and it is not to be expected that in his youth he should
be emancipated from the errors of his time. But this
unjust picture has given Schlegel occasion to say that
'the wonderful saviour of her country, Joan of Arc, is
portrayed by Shakespeare with an Englishman's prejudices.'   History has since done justice to her
memory, and time has found the solution of her supposed miraculous influence.   The inhabitants of the
little hamlet where she was born were remarkable for
their simplicity and their superstition ; and the poor
peasant girl, whom a pious education had ripened into
a religious enthusiast, was led, while tending her flocks
in solitude among the hills and pastures of a wild and
picturesque country, to occupy herself with day-dreams
concerning the ascetic and miraculous lives of the
saints, and the wonderful heroism of the virgin martyrs.   This sort of life led to its natural result in a
fervent and susceptible mind ; after a short time she
was haunted by visions, and listened in ecstasy to the
voices of spirits ; angelic faces appeared to her surrounded by a halo of light and glory ; amongst them
were St. Catherine and St. Margaret, wearing crowns
which glittered with celestial jewels, and these heavenly
visitants spoke to her in voices which were sweeter
than the softest music.   They commanded her to
deliver her country, and told her that she would be
endowed with strength from heaven. The devoted
enthusiast went to the king, declared her mission,
liberated France, and was finally, with a cruelty at
which humanity recoils, burnt at the stake for sorcery.
It is to be wished that Shakespeare had taken a more

lofty and generous view of her character   The family of this unhappy woman was ennobled by the monarch to whom she had rendered such important services, but he made no effort whatever to rescue from the hands of the English a heroine 'to whom the more generous superstition of the ancients would have erected altars '

Viewed historically, there are some slight apologies to be made for the conduct of York in attempting to supplant Henry on the throne , but in the drama he stands convicted of complicated treachery and constant perjury.   The feeble but generous king restores him to his rank and estates, which had been forfeited by the treason of his father, who was beheaded for a plot to assassinate Henry the Fifth.   He promises eternal gratitude and allegiance, exclaiming—

> And so thrive Richard as thy foes may fall!
> And as my duty springs, so perish they
> That grudge one thought against your majesty!

Yet this very man, perceiving the imbecility of Henry, casts an evil eye unto the crown, and eventually he and his sons, after shedding the blood of nearly a hundred thousand Englishmen, exterminate the house of Lancaster, and place the sensual, perjured Edward upon the throne.

In the early part of the play the young king does not appear, and when he does, it is only to make a miserable exhibition of his weakness and vacillation of mind , for, although contracted to another lady, he falls in love with Margaret merely from Suffolk's description of her personal charms, and thus becomes the dupe of that cunning courtier, who loves her him-

23

self. The play ends abruptly with Henry's dispatching Suffolk to France to woo Margaret for him, and the wily emissary speeds on his mission rejoicing in the probable success of his treachery.

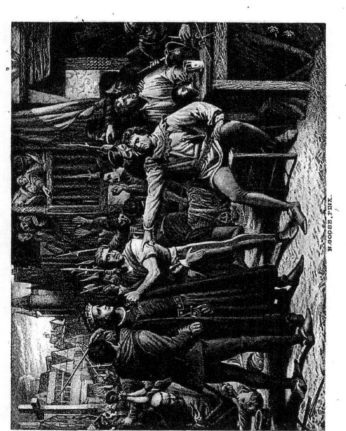

M.GOODE, PINX.

JACK CADE AND LORD SAY.

Second Part of King Henry VI. Act IV. Scene VII.

HISTORICAL SUMMARY OF 'KING HENRY VI.'—PART II.

An old play in two parts, which appears to have been written about the year 1590, and which is ascribed by Malone to the pen of Christopher Marlowe, assisted by his friends Poole and Greene, is the foundation of this and the ensuing drama, the prototype of the present being called 'The First Part of the Contention of the two famous Houses of Yorke and Lancaster.' These two parts were published in quarto, the first in 1594, the second in the following year: both were reprinted in 1600, and seem to have been moulded by our author, with many alterations and additions. into the shape in which they at present appear

The action of this drama comprises ten years, commencing with Henry's marriage with Margaret of Anjou, in May, 1445, and terminating with the first battle of Saint Albans, in favor of the house of York, May 22, 1455

PERSONS REPRESENTED.

King Henry the Sixth.
Humphrey, duke of Gloster, his uncle
Cardinal Beaufort, bishop of Winchester, great uncle to the king.

RICHARD PLANTAGENET, duke of York.
EDWARD and RICHARD, his sons
DUKE OF SOMERSET,
DUKE OF SUFFOLK,
DUKE OF BUCKINGHAM,   } of the king's party.
LORD CLIFFORD,
YOUNG CLIFFORD, his son,
EARL OF SALISBURY,
EARL OF WARWICK,   } of the York faction
LORD SCALES, governor of the Tower   LORD SAY.
SIR HUMPHREY STAFFORD, and his brother.   SIR
    JOHN STANLEY.
A SEA CAPTAIN, MASTER and MASTER'S MATE, and
    WALTER WHITMORE
TWO GENTLEMEN, prisoners with Suffolk
A HERALD   VAUX.
HUME and SOUTHWELL, two priests
BOLINGBROKE, a conjurer.   A Spirit raised by him
THOMAS HORNER, an armorer   PETER, his man
CLERK OF CHATHAM.   MAYOR OF SAINT ALBANS.
SIMPCOX, an impostor   TWO MURDERERS
JACK CADE, a rebel.
GEORGE, JOHN, DICK, SMITH the weaver, MICHAEL,
    etc., his followers
ALEXANDER IDEN, a Kentish gentleman.

MARGARET, queen to King Henry.
ELEANOR, duchess of Gloster
MARGERY JOURDAIN, a witch.   WIFE TO SIMPCOX

Lords, Ladies, and Attendants; Petitioners, Alder-
    men, a Beadle, Sheriff, and Officers, Citizens, Pren-
    tices, Falconers, Guards, Soldiers, Messengers, etc

SCENE, dispersedly in various parts of England.

COMPENDIUM OF THE PLAY.

THE nuptials of King Henry VI. with Margaret of Anjou are scarcely celebrated, in the 24th year of the king, when the new queen resolves to exercise unlimited control over the councils of her imbecile husband, and with the assistance of a number of powerful nobles, to remove the duke of Gloster from his post of protector Their purpose is at length effected, and the virtuous duke confined on a charge of high treason His accusers, perceiving the evidence of his guilt insufficient to obtain the least credit, have recourse to assassination The populace, driven to desperation at the murder of their patron, tumultuously insist on the immediate banishment of Suffolk, his avowed enemy, who, in his passage to France, is captured by pirates and beheaded. In the meantime the government of Ireland is intrusted to the duke of York, who previous to his departure induces a needy dependent, named Cade, to commence an insurrection in Kent, laying claim to the crown as a descendant of Edmund Mortimer, in order that he may thereby be enabled to judge of the probability of his own success Cade and his party are at length dispersed by the king's forces, and the duke of York soon after arrives in England to support his pretensions to the throne by force of arms. The hostile parties come to a general engagement near Saint Albans, where the Lancastrians sustain a total defeat, and the victorious duke resolves to commence his march to the capital without delay

In perusing this play we seem to be walking among covered pitfalls, the snares of treachery are spread in all directions; every noble is striving for supremacy, and each exclaiming on the ambition of the rest. The drama forms a dark and terrible picture of the wickedness of courts; for sophistry, perjury and murder stain nearly every character except the weak king and the 'good Duke Humphrey.' We recoil in disgust from this diabolical exhibition of state-craft these wily courtiers play for the crown of the feeble Henry with all the recklessness of ruined gamblers, they stake body and soul upon the cast, or rather play as if they had no souls to lose. The poet, with all the ingenuity of youth, scourges hypocrisy with unsparing vehemence, treachery is made transparent, and the great struggle for self rendered obvious and disgusting, he tears aside the disguises of patriotism and religion, and shows us the human fiends concealed beneath them.

The character of the king is very weak, and the feebleness of infancy had not given way to the strength and vigor of manhood, and the son of that determined prince, who was regarded by the people with affectionate awe, was a gentle, weak, superstitious man. As a village priest he would have proved a valuable member of society, happy would it have been for him and England had he been born to such a station; but as a king who had to govern a powerful and insolent nobility, and a semi-barbarous people, his very virtues were his chief defects. In those times a strong bad man, so that he had judgment enough not to stretch his prerogative too far, made a better sovereign than a weak good man. Where much power attaches to the crown, a feeble king is worse than no king, for the powers of government are wielded by any hand that is bold enough to seize them and strong enough to guide them. Thus with Henry—Gloucester, Beaufort, Suffolk, Somerset, York, and Warwick, each in turn influence and coerce this phantom of a king The mind of the unfortunate monarch was worse than feeble , it was diseased. He was several times seized with an extraordinary apathy and imbecility, which rendered him unfit for the commonest duties of life, and unconscious of the presence or inquiries of his friends , but Shakespeare has not alluded to this mental defect in his portraiture of the unhappy king

Margaret of Anjou was selected by the cardinal and his compeers for Henry as a wife calculated to rouse him into greater activity, and to impart to him some of the decision of character and strength of mind that she possessed Added to great personal beauty and remarkable vivacity, she had a courageous temper and masculine intellect, and was regarded as the most accomplished woman of her age Her pride and vindictiveness of temper she had not yet revealed ; no royal state or adverse fortune had called them into activity , the young beauty had lived in comparative seclusion, adding accomplishments to natural graces, and it was thought, with much probability, that when she shared the throne of Henry, she would increase its lustre and elevate the character of its occupant Had her husband possessed a sounder judgment, and a royalty of nature she would doubtless have fulfilled these hopes respecting her, but Margaret had no one whose influence could restrain in her those arbitrary doctrines which she had learnt in France and attempted to apply in England. She was distinguished by a haughtiness greater than had hitherto been assumed by any of their native kings, and she sank into unpopularity and dislike.

HISTORICAL SUMMARY OF 'KING HENRY VI.'—PART III.

THE second part of the old drama which supplied our author with materials for the present production is entitled 'The true Tragedie of Richarde Duke of Yorke, and the Death of good King Henrie the Sixt; with the whole Contention between the two Houses Lancaster and Yorke, as it was sundry times acted by the Right Honorable the Earle of Pembrooke his servants' Both this and the preceding play were reprinted together in 1600, which Malone considers as a strong proof that they cannot be ascribed to the author of the first part of this sovereign's history.

The present historical drama was altered by Crowne, and brought on the stage in the year 1680, under the title of 'The Miseries of Civil War.' The works of Shakespeare could have been little read at that period; for the author, in his prologue, declares the play to be entirely his own composition; whereas the very first scene is that of Jack Cade, copied almost *verbatim* from the 'Second Part of King Henry VI' and several others from his Third Part with as little variation

The action of this play comprehends a period of sixteen years It commences with the events immediately succeeding the first battle of Saint Albans in 1455, and concludes with the murder of King Henry VI and the birth of Prince Edward, afterwards Edward V., in 1471

'Of these three plays,' says Dr. Johnson, 'I think

M. ADAMO, PINX.

WARWICK AND KING EDWARD.

Third Part of King Henry VI. Act IV. Scene III.

the second the best.' The truth is, that they have not
sufficient variety of action, for the incidents are too
often of the same kind, yet many of the characters
are well discriminated   King Henry and his queen,
King Edward, the duke of Gloster, and the earl of
Warwick are very strongly and distinctly painted.

PERSONS REPRESENTED.

KING HENRY THE SIXTH
EDWARD, prince of Wales, his son
LEWIS XI, king of France
DUKE OF SOMERSET,
DUKE OF EXETER,
EARL OF OXFORD,   lords on King Henry's
EARL OF NORTHUMBERLAND,   side
EARL OF WESTMORELAND,
LORD CLIFFORD,
RICHARD PLANTAGENET, duke of York
EDWARD, earl of March, afterwards King
    Edward IV,
EDMUND, earl of Rutland,   his sons
GEORGE, afterwards duke of Clarence,
RICHARD, afterwards duke of Gloster,
DUKE OF NORFOLK,
MARQUIS OF MONTAGUE,
EARL OF WARWICK,   of the duke of York's
EARL OF PEMBROKE,   party.
LORD HASTINGS,
LORD STAFFORD,

SIR JOHN MORTIMER, ⎫
SIR HUGH MORTIMER, ⎬ uncles to the duke of York
HENRY, earl of Richmond, a youth
LORD RIVERS, brother to lady Grey   SIR WILLIAM
    STANLEY.   SIR JOHN MONTGOMERY.   SIR JOHN
    SOMERVILLE   TUTOR to Rutland.   MAYOR OF
    YORK.   LIEUTENANT OF THE TOWER   A NOBLE-
    MAN.   TWO KEEPERS   A HUNTSMAN   A Son
    that has killed his father   A Father that has
    killed his son

QUEEN MARGARET.
LADY GREY, afterwards queen to Edward IV
BONA, sister to the French queen

Soldiers and other Attendants on King Henry and
    King Edward, Messengers, Watchmen, etc

SCENE, during part of the third act, in France; during
    all the rest of the play, in England

COMPENDIUM OF THE PLAY.

THE duke of York enters London in triumph, and
extorts from the imbecile Henry a recognition of his
succession to the throne in return for an undisturbed
possession of his regal dignity during life   The con-
flicting interests of each party soon lead to an infraction
of this treaty : Richard is defeated and taken prisoner
in a battle near Wakefield in Yorkshire, and soon after
put to death, while the infant duke of Rutland, his
son, is barbarously murdered in cold blood by Lord

Clifford. The powerful assistance of the earl of Warwick enables the depressed Yorkists in their turn to defeat their opponents at Towton in Yorkshire, and place Edward duke of York on the throne King Henry escapes to Scotland, but is at length committed to the Tower, while his queen and son repair to Paris to implore the aid of the French king, whose sympathy is weakened by the presence of Warwick, who is commissioned by his master to solicit the hand of the princess Bona, the sister of Lewis ; when a messenger from England suddenly arrives with the intelligence of Edward's marriage with Lady Elizabeth Grey. Exasperated at this insult, Warwick forms a treaty of alliance with Margaret and Lewis, and speedily dethrones his sovereign, who effects his escape to Burgundy, where he obtains a supply of troops, and soon after lands at Ravensburg a great number of his adherents flock to his standard, and Warwick is routed and slain in a general engagement near Barnet A still more decisive action at Tewkesbury destroys the relics of the Lancastrian forces the prince of Wales is stabbed to the heart by the three royal brothers in the presence of his mother , while the captive monarch is himself assassinated in the Tower by Richard, duke of Gloster.

HISTORICAL SUMMARY OF 'KING RICHARD III'

SHAKESPEARE'S historical authorities in the composition of this popular drama were the 'History of Richard the Third' by Sir Thomas More, and its continuation in the 'Chronicles of Holinshed.' The date of 1593 is the period assigned by Malone to its production, which however was not entered at Stationers' Hall till 1597.

The reign of Richard III appears to have been a favorite subject of dramatists and other poets who preceded our author; but no sufficient evidence has been produced that Shakespeare borrowed from any of them Mr Boswell indeed supposed that an old play, published in 1594, 'An Enterlude, intitled the Tragedie of Richard the Third, wherein is showne the deathe of Edward the Fourthe, with the smotheringe of the two princes in the Tower, with the lamentable ende of Shore's wife, and the contention of the two houses of Lancaster and Yorke,'—had so great a resemblance to this play, that the author must have seen it before he composed his own. It is, notwithstanding, one of the worst of the ancient dramas, and bears but few traces of general likeness

The historical events here recorded occupy a space of about fourteen years, but are frequently confused for the purposes of dramatic representation. The second scene of the first act commences with the fu-

R.GOOSE. PINX.

KING RICHARD III.

Act II., Scene IV.

neral of King Henry VI, who is said to have been murdered on the 21st of May, 1471, while the imprisonment of Clarence, which is represented previously in the first scene, did not take place till 1477–8

In speaking of this play, Dr Johnson remarks: 'This is one of the most celebrated of our author's performances, yet I know not whether it has not happened to him as to others, to be praised most when praise is not most deserved. That this play has scenes noble in themselves, and very well contrived to strike on the exhibition, cannot be denied; but some parts are trifling, others shocking, and some improbable.'

PERSONS REPRESENTED.

KING EDWARD THE FOURTH
EDWARD, prince of Wales, afterwards ⎫
    King Edward V.,   ⎬ sons to the king.
RICHARD, duke of York,   ⎭
GEORGE, duke of Clarence,   ⎫
RICHARD, duke of Gloster, afterwards ⎬ brothers to the king
    King Richard III,   ⎭
A young SON of Clarence
HENRY, earl of Richmond, afterwards King Henry VII
CARDINAL BOURCHIER, archbishop of Canterbury
THOMAS ROTHERAM, archbishop of York.
JOHN MORTON, bishop of Ely.
DUKE OF BUCKINGHAM
DUKE OF NORFOLK.   EARL OF SURREY, his son.

EARL RIVERS, brother to King Edward's queen
MARQUIS OF DORSET and LORD GREY, her sons.
EARL OF OXFORD   LORD HASTINGS   LORD STAN-
    LEY   LORD LOVEL
SIR THOMAS-VAUGHN   SIR RICHARD RATCLIFF
SIR WILLIAM CATESBY   SIR JAMES TYRREL
SIR JAMES BLOUNT   SIR WALTER HERBERT
SIR ROBERT BRAKENBURY, lieutenant of the Tower.
CHRISTOPHER URSWICK, a Priest   Another Priest
LORD MAYOR OF LONDON   SHERIFF OF WILTSHIRE

ELIZABETH, queen of King Edward IV
MARGARET, widow of King Henry VI
DUCHESS OF YORK, mother to King Edward IV.
    Clarence and Gloster
LADY ANNE, widow of Edward, prince of Wales, son
    to King Henry VI , afterwards married to the
    duke of Gloster
A young DAUGHTER of Clarence.

Lords, and other Attendants , two Gentlemen , a Pur-
    suivant, Scrivener, Citizens, Murderers, Messen-
    gers, Ghosts, Soldiers, etc

SCENE, England

COMPENDIUM OF THE PLAY

THE extinction of the house of Lancaster and the
declining health of the king induce Richard, duke of
Gloster, to commence his career of ambition with the

removal of the duke of Clarence, who is privately assassinated in prison by his orders Edward shortly after expires, leaving Richard protector of the realm, who immediately withdraws the two young princes from the superintendence of their maternal relatives . these unfortunate noblemen are executed on a pretended discovery of treason , a similar fate awaits Lord Hastings for his fidelity to the legitimate successor of his deceased master , while the innocent children are conveyed to the Tower By the powerful assistance of the duke of Buckingham, Richard obtains the crown, which is followed by the murder of his nephews in the Tower, and the poisoning of his wife, in order to facilitate an alliance with his niece, which he hopes to accomplish by the aid of her mother These events are succeeded by the defection and execution of the duke of Buckingham In the meantime, Henry, earl of Richmond, having assembled a large army, embarks at Bretagne, and lands at Milford Haven he resolves to proceed towards the capital without delay, and reaches the town of Bosworth in Leicestershire, where he is encountered by the forces of the usurper, who is defeated and slain , while the regal dignity devolves on his fortunate rival, who assumes the title of Henry VII and puts a period to the long contention between the rival families by an immediate union with Elizabeth, the daughter of Edward IV.

The part of Richard is, perhaps beyond all others, variegated, and consequently favorable to a judicious performer It comprehends, indeed, a trait of almost every character on the stage the hero, the lover, the statesman, the buffoon, the hypocrite, the hardened and repenting sinner, etc , are to be found within its compass. No wonder, therefore, that the discriminating powers of a Burbagé, a Garrick and a Henderson, Booth, Cook, Kean, Phelps and Irving should at different periods have given it a popularity beyond other dramas of the same author.

F.PECHT.PINX.

WOOLSEY, KING HENRY VIII. AND ANNE BULLEN.

King Henry VIII. Act I. Scene IV.

HISTORICAL SUMMARY OF 'KING HENRY VIII'

THIS drama is conjectured by Malone to have been written a short time previous to the death of Queen Elizabeth, which happened March 24, 1602–3, as well from the prophetic eulogium on that princess in the last scene, as from the imperfect manner in which the panegyric on her successor is connected with the foregoing and subsequent lines   After having been laid aside for several years, it is said to have been revived at the Globe Theatre, June 29, 1613, under the title of 'All is True,' with new decorations, and a prologue and epilogue   During this representation, the theatre accidentally caught fire, occasioned by the discharge of some small pieces, called chambers, on King Henry's arrival at Cardinal Wolsey's gate at Whitehall, one of which being injudiciously managed, set fire to the thatched roof of the building, which was entirely consumed

Unlike the other English historical plays of Shakespeare, 'Henry the Eighth' had no predecessors on the stage   The pages of history alone furnish materials for its composition, and there are few passages throughout the play which cannot be traced to Fox's 'Acts and Monuments of Christian Martyrs,' or to Cavendish's 'Life of Wolsey,' as found in the 'Chronicles of Holinshed'   The action comprises a period of twelve years, commencing in 1521, the twelfth year of
24

King Henry's reign, and ending with the baptism of Elizabeth in 1533 It should be observed, however, that Queen Katharine did not die until January 8, 1536.

'This play,' says Dr Johnson, 'is one of those which still keep possession of the stage by the splendor of its pageantry yet pomp is not its only merit. The meek sorrows and virtuous distress of Katharine have furnished some scenes which may be justly numbered among the greatest efforts of tragedy but the genius of Shakespeare comes in and goes out with Katharine Every other part may be easily conceived and easily written.'

PERSONS REPRESENTED

KING HENRY THE EIGHTH
CARDINAL WOLSEY.   CARDINAL CAMPEIUS
CAPUCIUS, ambassador from the emperor, Charles V.
CRANMER, archbishop of Canterbury
DUKE OF NORFOLK   DUKE OF BUCKINGHAM.
DUKE OF SUFFOLK   EARL OF SURREY.
LORD CHAMBERLAIN.   LORD CHANCELLOR
GARDINER, bishop of Winchester.
BISHOP OF LINCOLN   LORD ABERGAVENNY   LORD
    SANDS
SIR HENRY GUILDFORD   SIR THOMAS LOVELL.
SIR ANTHONY DENNY   SIR NICHOLAS VAUX.
SECRETARIES to Wolsey.
CROMWELL, servant to Wolsey.
GRIFFITH, gentleman usher to Queen Katharine.

THREE OTHER GENTLEMEN.
DOCTOR BUTTS, physician to the king.
GARTER, king at arms.
SURVEYOR to the duke of Buckingham.
BRANDON, and a SERGEANT at arms.
DOORKEEPER of the council chamber   PORTER, and
    his MAN.
PAGE to Gardiner   A CRIER.

QUEEN KATHARINE, wife to King Henry . afterwards
    divorced.
ANNE BULLEN, her maid of honor , afterwards queen.
AN OLD LADY, friend to Anne Bullen
PATIENCE, woman to Queen Katharine

Several Lords and Ladies in the dumb shows , Women
    attending upon the queen , Spirits, which appear
    to her , Scribes, Officers, Guards and other At-
    tendants.

SCENE, chiefly in London and Westminster ; once, at
    Kimbolton.

COMPENDIUM OF THE PLAY.

THE duke of Buckingham imprudently involves
himself in personal hostilities with Cardinal Wolsey,
who finds means of seducing the confidential servants
of his rival, and convicting him of high treason   The
king shortly after becomes violently enamored of a
young lady named Anne Bullen, the power of whose
attractions contributes to increase the conscientious

scruples which he had previously entertained of the legality of his marriage with Queen Katharine, the widow of his deceased brother. The cardinal, apprehensive of his master's union with one who is suspected to favor the principles of the Reformation, sends private instructions to the papal court, to whose decision Queen Katharine had appealed, that the sentence of divorce may be delayed   This letter, together with an inventory of his enormous wealth, falls by mistake into the hands of the enraged monarch, who immediately deprives Wolsey of all his civil offices , and the fallen favorite is only saved from a charge of high treason by the timely interposition of death   The new queen is now crowned with great magnificence, while her amiable predecessor dies of a broken heart. In the meantime a conspiracy is formed against Archbishop Cranmer, who is enabled to triumph over the malice of his powerful enemies by the favor of the king   The play concludes with the baptism of the infant Elizabeth, the glories of whose future reign, and those of her successor, are prophetically foretold by Cranmer, who is appointed by Henry as sponsor to the princess.

J.C.ARMYTAGE, PINX.

TROILUS AND CRESSIDA.

Act III. Scene II.

HISTORICAL SUMMARY OF 'TROILUS AND CRESSIDA'

THE composition of this play is attributed by Malone to the date of 1602 That it was written and acted before the decease of Queen Elizabeth is evident from the manner in which it is entered or the Stationers' books, being registered on February 7, 1602–3, 'as acted by my lord chamberlein's men,' who, in the vear of the accession of King James, obtained a license for their theatre, and were denominated 'his majesty's servants '

Chaucer had celebrated the loves of Troilus and Cressida in a translation from a Latin poem of one Lollius, an old Lombard author but Shakespeare is supposed to have received the greatest part of his materials for the structure of this drama fiom Guido of Columpna, a native of Messina in Sicily, who wrote his ' History of Troy' in Latin This work appears to have been soon after translated by Raoul le Fevre into French, from whom Caxton rendered it into English in 1471, under the title of ' Recuyles, or Destruction of Troy ' Our author has in his stoi y followed, for the greater part, the old book of Caxton, which was then very popular ; but the character of Thersites, of which it makes no mention, is a proof that this play was written after Chapman had published his version of Homer in 1596.

PERSONS REPRESENTED.

PRIAM, king of Troy.

HECTOR,
TROILUS,
PARIS,   } his sons.
DEIPHOBUS,
HELENUS,

ÆNEAS,   } Trojan commanders
ANTENOR,

CALCHAS, a Trojan priest, taking part with the Greeks.
PANDARUS, uncle to Cressida
MARGARELON, a bastard son of Priam

AGAMEMNON, the Grecian general
MENELAUS, his brother.

ACHILLES,
AJAX,
ULYSSES,
NESTOR,   } Grecian commanders
DIOMEDES,
PATROCLUS,

THERSITES, a deformed and scurrilous Grecian
ALEXANDER, servant to Cressida
Servant to Troilus, Servant to Paris, Servant to Diomedes

HELEN, wife to MENELAUS
ANDROMACHE, wife to Hector.
CASSANDRA, daughter to Priam; a prophetess.
CRESSIDA, daughter to Calchas

Trojan and Greek Soldiers and Attendants.

SCENE, Troy, and the Grecian camp before it

COMPENDIUM OF THE PLAY.

CALCHAS, a Trojan priest of Apollo, deserts the
cause of his country, and traitorously joins the camp
of the Grecians, to whom he renders most important
services, in recompense of which he intercedes for the
ransom of a powerful Trojan captive named Antenor,
in exchange for his daughter Cressida, who resides in
Troy, under the protection of her uncle Pandarus, where
her beauty and accomplishments make a deep impression on prince Troilus, the son of king Priam, whose addresses she is induced to accept, when their felicity is
suspended by the arrival of Diomed, who is commissioned to effect the exchange and restore Cressida to
her father. Vows of mutual fidelity are interchanged
by the separated lovers, and Troilus soon finds an opportunity to repair secretly to the Grecian tents, where
he has the mortification of witnessing the inconstancy
of his mistress, who has transferred her affections to
Diomed In the meantime, Hector, disregarding the
predictions of his sister Cassandra, and the entreaties
of his wife Andromache, repairs to the field of battle,
where he slays Patroclus, the friend of Achilles, who
soon after revenges his death on his conqueror, whose
dead body he cruelly attaches to his chariot which he
drives round the walls of the city.

The destruction of Troy would have been a theme
worthy of the pen of Shakespeare, had he confined
his overflowing and sometimes erratic genius to his
subject, he had admirable materials in his hand, had
he attempted less. The play abounds with characters,
but they are introduced and then abandoned before

we are fairly acquainted with them they vanish   Cressida is little more than a sketch, and Cassandra, the
mad prophetess, something less than one   The best
developed character is Pandarus, and he is altogether
contemptible.   Thersites is probably the original of
Apemantus, there is, at least, a resemblance between
them, but the latter is the most finished character.
Shakespeare apparently intended to create a sympathy
and admiration for Troilus, for he makes 'that same
dog-fox, Ulysses,' speak eloquently in his favor, com-
paring him with Hector, and declaring that he was—

'Not yet mature, yet matchless; firm of word;
Speaking in deeds, and deedless in his tongue;
Not soon provoked, nor, being provoked, soon calmed;
His heart and hand both open and both free'

Still, a mere lover is generally an insipid creation, and
Troilus is scarcely an exception to the rule, he wants
purpose, decision, and moral courage   The conduct
of Pandarus is mean and officious enough, but Troilus
shares his shame by employing him.   Cressida was
open to be wooed, and easy to be won ; she is sufficiently
complying, in all conscience, and only retires when
she is feebly pursued.   Had Troilus won her in an
open, manly manner, he would probably have preserved both her affection and her honor.   Fanciful,
giddy coquette as she is, she would have remained
virtuous, had she not encountered temptation

But the play is full of fine poetry and profound ob-
servations ; if we are for a moment angry with Shakespeare for his wanderings or his inconsistency, he soon
wins us back to him with bribes of thought and
beauty   The play also has many fine scenes, for instance, that between Cressida and her uncle, in the

first act, is remarkable for sparkling dialogue; the
same may be said of the first scene of the second act,
between the savage jester Thersites and the blunt
Ajax.   The short scene in the third act, where Helen
is introduced, is exceedingly natural and lively, the
equivocations of the servant whom Pandarus addresses
are fully as humorous as the sayings of the licensed
fools in other of our poet's plays   The scene in the
garden of Pandarus, where the lovers meet and confess their affection, is exceedingly beautiful, we are
reminded for a moment of a similar scene in 'Romeo
and Juliet,' but the resemblance soon ceases—the passionate though chaste and womanly affection of Juliet,
compared to the wanton appetite of Cressida, is as a
pure bright star in heaven to the cold delusive fire
which dances in darkness over the stagnant pool or
trackless marsh   The dialogue between Achilles and
Hector after the tournament is in Shakespeare's hap-
piest style   The bulky Achilles, scanning the Trojan
prince with his eyes, and soliciting the gods to tell him
in what part of his body he should destroy great Hector, is the sublime of chivalry.   Hector's passionate
rejoinder,

> 'Henceforth, guard thee well,
> For I'll not kill thee there, nor there, nor there,
> But, by the forge that stithed Mars his helm,
> I'll kill thee everywhere, yea, o'er and o'er,'

is equally fine, while the whole of the fifth act is
full of vigor and bustle, and exceedingly animated.

HISTORICAL SUMMARY OF 'TIMON OF ATHENS.'

No printed edition anterior to the folio of 1623 has yet been discovered of this tragedy, which abounds with perplexed, obscure and corrupt passages The year 1610 is conjectured by Malone as the most probable date of its production, while Dr Drake and Mr Chalmers suppose it to have been written as early as 1601 or 1602

Shakespeare is thought to have derived some of his materials for this drama from the perusal of a novel in Painter's 'Palace of Pleasure,' and from a very slight notice of Timon in Plutarch's 'Life of Antony,' translated by Sir Thomas North.   The late celebrated engraver, Mr. Strutt, had, however, a manuscript play on this subject, which appeared to have been written or transcribed about the year 1600, in which was a scene resembling Timon's feast in the third act of this drama , though, instead of warm water, the guests are served with stones painted like artichokes, with which they are driven out of the room · which incident our author is supposed to have had in mind when he made his fourth lord say,

'One day he gives us diamonds, next day stones.'

In the old play Timon then retires to the woods, attended by his faithful steward Laches, who disguises himself that he may continue his services to his master ,

PAINE, PINX.

GEORGE BENNETT AS APEMANTUS.

Timon of Athens, Act I, Scene II.

and in the last act the recluse is followed by his incon-
stant mistress, Callimela, and others, who had heard
that he had discovered a treasure in digging; features
likewise adopted in the present tragedy, in which,
however, all these hints have been incomparably improved and expanded, the original being a very inferior production, though, from the Greek frequently
introduced, apparently the work of a scholar.

PERSONS REPRESENTED

TIMON, a noble Athenian

LUCIUS, ⎫
LUCULLUS, ⎬ lords, and flatterers of Timon.
SEMPRONIUS, ⎭

VENTIDIUS, one of Timon's false friends
APEMANTUS, a churlish philosopher
ALCIBIADES, an Athenian general
FLAVIUS, steward to Timon

FLAMINIUS, ⎫
LUCILIUS, ⎬ Timon's servants.
SERVILIUS, ⎭

CAPHIS, ⎫
PHILOTUS, ⎪
TITUS, ⎬ servants to Timon's creditors.
LUCIUS, ⎪
HORTENSIUS, ⎭

TWO SERVANTS of Varro, and the SERVANT of Isi-
    dore, two of Timon's creditors
CUPID and MASKERS   THREE STRANGERS

POET, PAINTER, JEWELLER and MERCHANT.
OLD ATHENIAN   PAGE   FOOL

PHRYNIA, }
TIMANDRA, } mistresses to Alcibiades

Other Lords, Senators, Officers, Soldiers, Thieves and
Attendants.

SCENE, Athens and the woods adjoining.

COMPENDIUM OF THE PLAY.

AN opulent citizen of Athens, named Timon, ex-
pends the whole of his possessions in the service of his
country and pretended friends, who enrich themselves
by encouraging the indiscriminate profusion of their
patron The approach of poverty and the desertion
of his flatterers at length open the eyes of the deluded
Timon, and he resolves to express his sense of their
ingratitude at a repast, where nothing is provided but
hot water, with which he besprinkles his affrighted
guests He now abjures all human intercourse, and
seeks an asylum in the woods, where he subsists on the
roots of the earth, in digging for which he discovers a
large treasure in gold This acquisition enables him
to reward the fidelity of his steward Flavius, who
adheres to the broken fortunes of his master, while a
considerable sum is appropriated to the service of
Alcibiades, who was at that period laying siege to
Athens, with the intention of chastising the arrogance
of the senate, which had ungratefully repaid his past

services by a sentence of perpetual exile The unfortunate misanthrope is soon after discovered in his cave dead, and the Athenians surrender their city, after procuring favorable terms from their appeased conqueror

The tragedy includes two incidents, each arising from a similar cause, the flight of Timon and the banishment of Alcibiades, let us now turn our attention to the latter Shakespeare also found his life in Plutarch, but the poet has not very fully elaborated the character of the Athenian general Alcibiades was famous for his great personal beauty, his stubborn and ambitious temper, his eloquence, craftiness and dissipation His resolution was strongly shown even in his boyhood, for it is related that on one occasion he was playing at dice with some other boys in the street, when a loaded wagon coming up interrupted the game, Alcibiades called to the driver to stop, as it was his turn to throw, but the man disregarded him and drove on, while the other boys got out of the way, Alcibiades, however, was not to be so readily overcome, for throwing himself flat upon his face directly before the wagon, he told the rustic to drive on if he pleased Upon this the man was so startled that he instantly stopped his horses, and the resolute boy got up and had his throw with the dice. Brought up in luxury and universally courted he gave way to every dissipation, but was still exceedingly attached to the philosopher Socrates

Shakespeare does not adhere to history respecting the cause of the banishment of Alcibiades He was accused of sacrilege towards the goddesses Ceres and Proserpine and condemned to death, but he saved himself by taking refuge among the Spartans; to whose hospitality he made a vile return by seducing the wife of their king Agis. After a life spent in dissipation, war and political intrigue, he was at length assassinated by a secret order of the magistrates of Sparta. He was at that time living in a small village in Phrygia with his mistress Timandra His murderers surrounded the house at night and set it on fire, and on his issuing out, sword in hand, they fled to a distance and slew him with their darts and arrows He was buried by Timandra as honorably as her circumstances would permit

MAYALL, PINX.

MR. VANDENHOFF AS CORIOLANUS.

Coriolanus, Act II, Scene III.

HISTORICAL SUMMARY OF 'CORIOLANUS.'

THIS play was neither entered in the books of the Stationers' Company, nor printed, till the year 1623, when it appeared in the folio edition of Heminge and Condell From a slight resemblance between the language of the fable told by Menenius in the first scene, and that of the same apologue in 'Camden's Remains,' published in 1605, Malone supposes the passage to have been imitated from that volume He assigns the production, however, to 1609 or 1610, partly because most of the other plays of Shakespeare have been reasonably referred to other years, and therefore the present might be most naturally ascribed to a time when he had not ceased to write, and was probably unemployed, and partly from the mention of the mulberry by Volumnia, the white species of which fruit was brought into England in great quantities in 1609, though possibly other sorts had been already planted here

A rigid adherence to historical truth is preserved in the characters and events of this drama Many of the principal speeches are copied from Plutarch's 'Life of Coriolanus,' as translated by Sir Thomas North The time of action comprehends a period of about four years, commencing with the secession to the Mons Sacer in the year of Rome 262, and ending with the death of Coriolanus, A U. C 266

PERSONS REPRESENTED

CAIUS MARCIUS CORIOLANUS, a noble Roman
TITUS LARTIUS, ⎫
COMINIUS,   ⎬ generals against the Volscians.
MENENIUS AGRIPPA, friend to Coriolanus.
SICINIUS VELUTUS, ⎫
JUNIUS BRUTUS,   ⎬ tribunes of the people.
YOUNG MARCIUS, son to Coriolanus
ROMAN HERALD
TULLUS AUFIDIUS, general of the Volscians.
LIEUTENANT to Aufidius.
CONSPIRATORS with Aufidius
CITIZEN of Antium.
TWO VOLSCIAN GUARDS

VOLUMNIA, mother to Coriolanus
VIRGILIA, wife to Coriolanus.
VALERIA, friend to Virgilia.
GENTLEWOMAN, attending Virgilia

Roman and Volscian Senators, Patricians, Ediles,
    Lictors, Soldiers, Citizens, Messengers, Servants to
    Aufidius, and other Attendants.

SCENE, partly in Rome, and partly in the territories
        of the Volscians and Antiates

COMPENDIUM OF THE PLAY

THE expulsion of the Tarquins from Rome is succeeded by a famine, during which the plebeians extort
from the weakness of the nobility a gratuitous distri-
bution of corn, together with the appointment of two
popular officers called tribunes to protect their interests from the alleged oppression of the patricians.
The haughty Coriolanus, by his opposition to these
concessions, renders himself highly unpopular his
civil defects are, however, soon after effaced by the
splendor of his military achievements, which are
rewarded by his appointment to the consulate by the
senate, whose choice is about to be ratified by the suf-
frages of the people, when the powerful influence of
the two tribunes procures his rejection The violence
of temper displayed by Coriolanus at this disappointment affords matter of triumph to his crafty adversaries, who condemn him to perpetual banishment by
a decree of the people Exasperated at this insult,
the illustrious exile repairs to the capital of the Volscians, who gladly aid him in his schemes of revenge
by investing him and their own general Aufidius with
a joint command, which speedily overcomes all opposition ; and the hostile occupation of Rome is expected
with terror by its affrighted citizens The conqueror,
in the meantime, refuses to listen to the most solemn
embassies of his countrymen, until his mother and
wife, accompanied by a deputation of eminent Roman
matrons, at length prevail on him to raise the siege.
The Volscian army soon after returns home, where
Coriolanus, while justifying his conduct to the senate,
25

is assassinated by a band of conspirators in the interest
of his colleague Aufidius

Coleridge says : 'This play illustrates the wonder-
fully philosophic impartiality of Shakespeare's poli-
tics ' The poet, however, shows himself something
of an aristocrat He seems to entertain a contempt
for the common order of people, and places them in a
very ridiculous light. The citizens are made mere
creatures of fear and contradiction, wafted about by
every wind, and won by every suppliant. More stress
is laid on the folly of the plebeii than on the vices
of the patricians , and if history has recorded the
former as fickle, it has not left the latter stainless.
Their courage and self-denial sometimes made them
regarded as demi-gods, but their vices sunk them below the brutes The Roman satirists give pictures
of life in the great city which fill modern readers with
disgust and loathing. Shakespeare laughs at the
people , but if he intended Coriolanus to represent
the principle of aristocracy, he places that in no very
attractive light

Some apologists for the turbulent character of Coriolanus have been found who urge the prejudices he had
derived from birth and education ; from the fact that
he was a spoiled child of fortune ; and because that,
in his day, there were no connecting links between the
higher and lower classes, by which they might become known to and respect each other , but these ex-
cuses fall very short of a reasonable defence of his
haughtiness.

Volumnia, also, has been much praised as a noble
character , but she possesses too much of the pride
and arrogance of her son, though his nature is certainly softened in her : she is an Amazonian scold,

that holds the lives of the Roman citizens in less estimation than a mere whim of her son's; when they have irritated him, she wishes that they may all hang and burn too She has more experience and wisdom than he; and though she despises and hates the people as much, she truly vaunts she has a brain 'that leads her use of anger to better advantage' The softer character of Virgilia shows pale beside her, but it is far more pleasing, the sound of flutes is sweeter than the clang of trumpets, and the tender solicitude of the wife more interesting than the stately ambition of the mother.

Menenius is something between a patrician and a buffoon; his connexions are aristocratic, but his sympathies are with the people Out of his love for Coriolanus he becomes his parasite, and is, in the end, treated by that proud and selfish man with insolence and ingratitude His application of the fable of the belly and its members to the mutiny of the citizens is apt enough but we see that, after all, he loves the poor rogues whom he traduces His great objects of abuse are the tribunes, but they show far more sense than he. they were chosen guardians of the liberty of the people, and in opposing Coriolanus in his attempt at arbitrary power they but performed their duty. To have done less would have proved them unworthy of their great trust.

HISTORICAL SUMMARY OF 'JULIUS CÆSAR.'

THE adventures of Julius Cæsar and his untimely death had occupied the pens of several of our early dramatic authors previous to the composition of this tragedy, which is conjectured by Malone to have made its appearance in 1607; about which period, William Alexander, afterwards earl of Sterline, published a tragedy on the same subject, in which the assassination of Cæsar, which is not exhibited, but related to the audience, forms the catastrophe of his piece. To none of these sources, however, so far as we are acquainted with them, does Shakespeare appear to have been at all indebted; whilst every scene of his play proclaims his obligations to Plutarch's Lives, then recently translated by Sir Thomas North This drama was neither entered at Stationers' Hall, nor printed before 1623; but a memorandum in the papers of the late Mr. George Vertue states that a play, called 'Cæsar's Tragedy,' was acted at court before April 10, 1613, which is supposed to have been the present piece; it being a frequent practice at that time to alter the name of our author's plays

The events contained in this drama commence with the festival of the Lupercalia, in February, A U C 709, and concludes with the defeat of Brutus and Cassius, about the end of October, A U C 711.

ROBERT DOWNING AS MARC ANTONY.

Julius Cæsar, Act III, Scene II.

PERSONS REPRESENTED

JULIUS CÆSAR
OCTAVIUS CÆSAR, MARCUS ANTONIUS, M. ÆMIL. LEPIDUS, triumvires after the death of Julius Cæsar
CICERO, PUBLIUS, POPILIUS LENA, senators.
MARCUS BRUTUS, CASSIUS, CASCA, TREBONIUS, LIGARIUS, DECIUS BRUTUS, METELLUS CIMBER, CINNA, conspirators against Julius Cæsar.
FLAVIUS and MARULLUS, tribunes.
ARTEMIDORUS, a sophist of Cnidos
A SOOTHSAYER
CINNA, a poet Another POET.
LUCILIUS, TITINIUS, MESSALA, YOUNG CATO and VOLUMNIUS, friends to Brutus and Cassius
VARRO, CLITUS, CLAUDIUS, STRATO, LUCIUS, DARDANIUS, servants to Brutus
PINDARUS, servant to Cassius

CALPHURNIA, wife to Cæsar.
PORTIA, wife to Brutus

Senators, Citizens, Guards, Attendants, etc.

SCENE, during a great part of the play, at Rome; afterwards at Sardis; and near Philippi.

COMPENDIUM OF THE PLAY.

THE defeat of the two sons of Pompey in Spain having extinguished all opposition, Cæsar returns in triumph to the city, in order to prepare for his Parthian expedition, previous to which he is anxious to assume the crown, which is publicly presented to him by Mark Antony at the festival of the Lupercalia Alarmed at this prospect of regal usurpation, a band of conspirators, with Brutus and Cassius at their head, resolve to emancipate their country from tyranny , and the conqueror is accordingly assassinated in the senate-house The humane though mistaken policy of Brutus preserves the life of Antony, who soon finds means to excite the populace in his favor, and expel the conspirators from Rome The endeavors of this profligate man to succeed to the despotism of his late master prove unsuccessful , and he is reluctantly compelled to admit Octavius Cæsar, and a powerful general named Lepidus, to a share of the government, with whom a triumvirate is at length formed After issuing a sanguinary proscription, in which Cicero is included, and witnessing the destruction of their domestic enemies, Octavius and Antony embark for Macedonia, in pursuit of Brutus and Cassius, who risk a general engagement near Philippi, in which the republican army is totally routed , while their daring leaders are reduced to the melancholy necessity of resorting to a voluntary death to escape the vengeance of their victorious opponents

Julius Cæsar was a character worthy of the closest analytical investigation by the master-mind of Shakespeare ; his attainment of power, and his great influence with the Roman people, was entirely attributable to his lofty talents and indomitable courage, his patience under toil, his industry in the pursuit of success, his wise deliberation, and the unshaken steadiness with which he carried out his wonderful resolutions, were the terror of his adversaries and the astonishment of the world

'Brutus,' says Mr Drake, 'the favorite of the poet, is brought forward, not only adorned with all the virtues attributed to him by Plutarch, but in order to excite a deeper interest in his favor, and to prove that not jealousy, ambition, or revenge, but unalloyed patriotism was the sole director of his conduct Our author has drawn him as possessing the utmost sweetness and gentleness of disposition, sympathizing with all that suffer, and unwilling to inflict pain, but from motives of the strongest moral necessity He has most feelingly and beautifully painted him in the relations of a master, a friend and a husband, his kindness to his domestics, his attachment to his friends and his love to Portia, demonstrating that nothing but a high sense of public duty could have induced him to lift his hand against Cæsar It is this struggle between the humanity of his temper, and his ardent and hereditary love of liberty, now threatened with extinction by the despotism of Cæsar, that gives to Brutus that grandeur of character, and that predominancy over his associates in purity of intention, which secured to him the admiration of his contemporaries, and to which posterity has done ample justice, through the medium of Shakespeare, who has placed the virtues of Brutus, and the contest in his bosom between private regard and patriotic duty, in the noblest light, wringing, even from the lips of his bitterest enemy, the fullest eulogium on the rectitude of his principles and the goodness of his heart.'

Cassius is a man of more worldly wisdom than Brutus; his great tact and knowledge of human nature is displayed in his remark to Antony, to reconcile him to the murder of Cæsar:

> 'Your voice shall be as strong as any man's
> In the disposing of new dignities.'

Many touches of this worldliness appear in him; he is eminently fitted for a conspirator, but is still noble. We feel that Mark Antony, in his hour of triumph, slanders the memory of Cassius, in attributing his conspiring against Cæsar merely to envy. The scene in the streets of Rome, where Cassius walks through the storm at night, amid the prodigies that foretell the death of the ambitious dictator, and bares his 'bosom to the thunder-stone,' is the sublime of tragedy: it raises our expectations to the highest pitch, and is a fitting prelude to the approaching catastrophe; when Cæsar, surrounded by fierce looks and glittering swords, and gashed with three-and-twenty hideous wounds, falls dead on the base of his rival's statue, which is bespattered with his blood, and is supposed to look down, with grim satisfaction, on the death of his destroyer. The following scene, where Brutus in his orchard meditates the death of Cæsar, is finer still: his struggle between tenderness and duty, his love for his friend and his love for his country, his high bearing to his fellow-conspirators, where he deprecates the necessity of an oath to bind just men 'that have spoke the word and will not palter,' and his generous yielding of the secret to his heroic and noble wife, are all pregnant with the vivid fire of genius, all point to Shakespeare as the master-bard, who with exquisite and unerring coloring has filled up the spirited sketches of Plutarch.

HISTORICAL SUMMARY OF 'ANTONY AND CLEOPATRA'

THE composition of this tragedy is assigned by Malone to the date of 1608, although no publication of it
has been hitherto discovered anterior to the folio edition of 1623 Some of its incidents are supposed to
have been borrowed from a production of Daniel,
called 'The Tragedie of Cleopatra,' which was entered
on the books of the Stationers' Company in the year
1593 The materials used by Shakespeare were derived
from North's translation of Plutarch ; and he appears
to have been desirous of introducing every incident
and person which he found recorded ; for when the
historian mentions his grandfather Lamprias as his
authority for his account of the entertainments of Antony at Alexandria ,—in the old copy of this play, in a
stage direction, in act 1 , scene 2, Lamprias, Rannius
and Lucilius enter with the rest, but sustain no share
in the dialogue. Of the three plays founded by our
author on the history of Plutarch this is the one in
which he has least indulged his fancy His adherence
to his authority is minute, and he bestowed little pains
in the adaptation of the history to the purposes of the
drama, beyond an ingenious and frequently elegant
metrical arrangement of the humble prose of North.
The action comprises the events of ten years, commencing with the death of Fulvia, B C 40, and termi-

MEETING OF ANTONY AND CLEOPATRA.

Antony and Cleopatra, Act II. Scene II.

O. WERTHEIMER, PINX.

nating with the final overthrow of the Ptolemean dynasty, B C 30

PERSONS REPRESENTED.

M Antony,
Octavius Cæsar, } triumvirs.
M Æmil Lepidus, }
Sextus Pompeius
Domitius Enobarbus, }
Ventidius, }
Eros, }
Scarus, - } friends of Antony.
Dercetas, }
Demetrius, }
Philo, }
Mecænas, }
Agrippa, }
Dolabella, }
Proculeius, } friends to Cæsar.
Thyreus, }
Gallus, }
Menas, }
Menecrates, } friends of Pompey.
Varrius, }
Taurus, lieutenant-general to Cæsar.
Canidius, lieutenant-general to Antony.
Silius, an officer in Ventidius's army.
Euphronius, an ambassador from Antony to Cæsar.
Alexas, Mardian, Seleucus and Diomedes, attendants on Cleopatra
Soothsayer. Clown.

CLEOPATRA, queen of Egypt.
OCTAVIA, sister to Cæsar, and wife to Antony.
CHARMIAN, ⎫
IRAS,   ⎬ attendants to Cleopatra.

Officers, Soldiers, Messengers and other Attendants
    SCENES in Alexandria and several parts of the
    Roman empire.

COMPENDIUM OF THE PLAY.

THE government of the eastern provinces, awarded
to Antony in the threefold partition of the Roman
empire, enables him to indulge without restraint his
natural taste for prodigality and dissipation, and the
duties of his high office are sacrificed at the shrine of
Cleopatra, whose influence is suspended by the mari-
time superiority of Sextus Pompeius, which recalls
her admirer to the capital   A family alliance is here
contracted with Octavia, the sister of Cæsar, who becomes the wife of Antony, and accompanies her husband to his seat of government, after the seeming
restoration of public tranquility.   The success of
Cæsar, who soon after defeats the forces of Pompey,
and deprives Lapidus of his share in the triumvirate,
at length alarms the effeminate Antony, who provokes
the resentment of his powerful rival by his desertion
of the amiable Octavia, and his renewed subjugation
to the charms of the Egyptian queen.   The hostile
fleets encounter near the promontory of Actium,
where the fortunes of Cæsar prevail, in consequence
of the perfidy of Cleopatra, who betakes herself to
flight in the midst of the action, and the infatuated

A. SPIESS. PINX.

DEATH OF CLEOPATRA.

Antony and Cleopatra. Act V. Scene II.

Antony, following her example, is compelled to avoid impending captivity by resorting to the alternative of a voluntary death; while Cleopatra is reserved to grace the triumph of her conqueror, whose vigilance she contrives to elude by depriving herself of life by the poison of asps, secretly conveyed to her in a basket of figs

In the play there are four characters which stand out prominently from the canvas—Cleopatra, Antony, Cæsar and Enobarbus. Of Cleopatra, as painted by the pencil of history, what a soft glow of voluptuous languor is thrown around her, and with what irresistible fascinations she is invested, the reader of the tragedy can alone feel and appreciate. Great as her faults are, for her life is but a tissue of refined and poetical sensuality, such is her devotion to Antony, and so winning is the gigantic extravagance of her affection for him, that we not only forgive her errors, but admire and applaud the actor of them

Antony and Cæsar are placed in strong contrast to each other; the one brave, reckless and prodigal, the other cool, prudent and avaricious. 'Cæsar gets money,' says Pompey, 'where he loses hearts.' Antony is a warrior and a prodigal, and Octavius a statesman, whose feelings are strictly under command. Something of predestination reigns through this play; everything tends towards the downfall of Antony and the advancement of Cæsar

Enobarbus, although an historical character, and to be found in Plutarch, does not there appear very prominently, and may, to no small extent, be called a creation of the pen of Shakespeare He found the name in history, but not the man he pictured Enobarbus forms one of the rich sunlights of the picture;

his plain bluntness has all the cheering hilarity of
comedy   But his jocularity would be out of place in
the latter scenes of the tragedy, how admirably does
Shakespeare obviate this   The dotage and ill-fortune
of Antony transform Enobarbus to a serious man, and
finally corrupt this hitherto faithful soldier; he deserts his master and flies to the service of Cæsar
The munificent Antony sends after him his chests and
treasure, which, in the hurry of flight, he had left
behind, this act of kindness strikes the penitent fugitive to the heart, and wasting in grief, he goes forth
to die, and alone, without the camp, breathing his
deep sorrow to the cold moon, does Enobarbus end his
life in the bitterness of despair

As his final ruin draws on, Antony is alternately
'valiant and dejected;' looking upon his high rank
and qualities, his unbounded but dazzling dissipation,
his imperial generosity, great personal courage, and
his gorgeous career; when hearing of his death, we
feel inclined to say with Cæsar

> 'The death of Antony
> Is not a single doom   in the name lay
> A moiety of the world'

That of Cleopatra follows; it is consistent with her
brilliant and luxurious life; she robs death of its
hideousness, and, enveloped in her royal robes and
crown, still radiant in that seductive beauty which
subdued Cæsar and ruined Antony, she applies to her
bosom the envenomed instrument of death, and falls
into an everlasting slumber 'as sweet as balm, as soft
as air,' where she yet looks .

> 'As she would catch another Antony
> In her strong toil of grace.'

A. LIEZENMAYER. PINX.

IACHIMO AND IMOGENE.

Cymbeline. Act II. Scene II.

HISTORICAL SUMMARY OF 'CYMBELINE'

THIS play is conjectured by Malone to have been
written in the year 1609, although it was neither entered on the books of the Stationers' Company nor
printed till 1623   The main incidents on which the
plot rests occur in a novel of Boccace ; but our author
is supposed to have derived them from an old story-
book popular in that age, entitled 'Westward for
Smelts'   All he knew of 'Cymbeline' he acquired
from Holinshed, who is sometimes closely followed,
and sometimes strangely perverted   This king, according to the old historian, succeeded his father in
the 19th year of the reign of Augustus , and the play
commences about the 24th year of Cymbeline's reign,
which was the 42d of the reign of Augustus and the
16th of the Christian era , notwithstanding which,
Shakespeare has peopled Rome with modern Italians,
Philario, Iachimo, etc   'Cymbeline' is said to have
reigned 35 years. leaving at his death two sons, Guiderius and Arviragus

This drama, if not in the construction of its fable,
one of the most perfect of our author's productions,
is, in point of poetic beauty, of variety and truth of
character, and in the display of sentiment and emo-
tion, one of the most interesting

PERSONS REPRESENTED.

CYMBELINE, king of Britain.

CLOTEN, son to the Queen by a former husband

LEONATUS POSTHUMUS, a gentleman, husband to Imogen

BELARIUS, a banished lord, disguised under the name of Morgan

GUIDERIUS, { sons to Cymbeline, disguised under the
ARVIRAGUS, { names of Polydore and Cadwal, supposed sons to Belarius.

PHILARIO, friend to Posthumus, } Italians.
IACHIMO, friend to Philario, } Italians.

FRENCH GENTLEMAN, friend to Philario

CAIUS LUCIUS, general of the Roman forces.

ROMAN CAPTAIN   TWO BRITISH CAPTAINS.

PISANIO, servant to Posthumus.

CORNELIUS, a physician.

TWO GENTLEMEN.

TWO JAILERS

QUEEN, wife to Cymbeline.

IMOGEN, daughter to Cymbeline by a former queen

HELEN, woman to Imogen

Lords, Ladies, Roman Senators, Tribunes, Apparitions, a Soothsayer, a Dutch Gentleman, a Spanish Gentleman, Musicians, Officers, Captains, Soldiers, Messengers and other Attendants

SCENE, sometimes in Britain, sometimes in Italy.

COMPENDIUM OF THE PLAY.

The Princess Imogen, only daughter of Cymbeline, king of Britain, secretly marries an accomplished courtier, named Posthumus, whose presumption is punished by a sentence of perpetual exile by the angry monarch. Deprived of the society of his amiable wife, the banished Posthumus repairs to Rome, where his confidence in the unshaken attachment of his princess is unhappily exchanged into a conviction of her infidelity by the false intelligence which he receives from Iachimo, a perfidious Italian; and the misguided husband immediately despatches orders to Pisanio, a faithful attendant residing in Britain, to put his mistress to death. Disregarding these cruel injunctions, Pisanio induces the unhappy lady to avoid the malice of her stepmother, and the importunities of her son Cloten, by flight. Disguised in male attire, Imogen arrives near Milford-haven, where she procures hospitable entertainment in the cottage of Belarius, a banished nobleman in the garb of a peasant, who had revenged the injuries which he had formerly sustained at the hands of Cymbeline, by stealing his two infant sons, and educating them as his own in this retreat. Cloten shortly after arrives in pursuit of Imogen, and is slain by the eldest of the princes in single combat. In the meantime, Posthumus and Iachimo accompany a Roman army to Britain, where Imogen, under the assumed name of Fidele, becomes a page to the Roman general, who sustains a signal defeat, in which the intrepid valor of Belarius and the two princes, assisted by Posthumus in the disguise of

26

a British soldier, is chiefly conspicuous Iachimo is taken prisoner, and makes a confession of his guilt to Cymbeline; Imogen is restored to her husband, Belarius pardoned, and the two princes publicly recognized, while the queen dies in despair at the loss of her son and the disappointment of her ambitious projects.

Our poet's object in writing this play was a noble one, the vindication of the character of woman from the lewd aspersions of thoughtless and unprincipled men It is not Imogen alone whom the Italian profligate, Iachimo, slanders—it is her whole sex, of his attempt upon her chastity, he says to her husband 'I durst attempt it against any lady in the world.' Impossible as it may appear to pure and innocent minds, men still live who are ignorant and sensual enough to make the same vile boast Among the pleasure-seeking gallants of that lascivious age, when seduction and duelling were by a large number of that class considered mere venial vices, if not graceful accomplishments, such unbelievers in the purity of woman were, perhaps, not uncommon, and in this play the bard read them a stern reproof from the stage.

Imogen is a personification of woman, woman enthroned in the holy temple of her pure and chaste affections, rejecting the tempter of her honor with the bitterest scorn and loathing, and enduring wrong and suffering with the most touching patience and sweetness The gentler sex should be always grateful to the memory of our great Shakespeare, for his genius did sweet homage to their character, he invests his female creations with all that is most pure and generous in humanity, picturing them, indeed, as beautiful to the eye, but a thousand times more acceptable to

the heart There is a moral dignity about his women,
a holy strength of affection, which neither suffering
nor death can pervert, that elevates them above the
sterner nature of man, placing them on an equality
with angels. The adventures of Imogen are like a
beautiful romance, her flight after her banished husband, her wretchedness and forlorn condition when
informed that he believes her false and has given
order for her death ; her assumption of boy's attire,
in which disguise she wanders among the mountains
at point to perish from hunger ; her meeting with her
disguised brothers in the cave ; her supposed death and
recovery, and, finally, her discovery of her repentant
husband, and throwing herself, without one reproach,
upon his bosom—are all beautifully portrayed Imogen is, indeed, a pattern of connubial love and chastity.

Posthumus is an irritable and impatient character ;
his love for Imogen is rather a selfish one, or he would
not have been so easily persuaded that she was false ;
it undergoes some purification in his trouble, and we
scarcely sympathize with him until his repentance of
his rashness He then doubts his own worthiness,
and feeling that he has wickedly presumed to direct
the wrath of Heaven and punish its offenders, exclaims ·

> ' Gods ' if you
> Should have ta'en vengeance on my faults, I never
> Had lived to put on this '

A reflection we all might advantageously make, when
contemplating revenge for any real or supposed injury.

Iachimo is an unconfirmed villain, as dishonest as
Iago, but not so devilish, for he has the grace to repent of his treachery ; he tries to compound with his
conscience, and satisfy it with flimsey sophistries.

He is ready to attest the truth of his false assertions with an oath, and does absolutely swear to Posthumus that he had the jewel from the arm of Imogen, which is literally true, but morally a perjury, because he stole the bracelet, and led the husband to suspect that it was given him in the gratification of an infamous affection Iachimo equivocates, Iago would have had no compunction about the matter, but have sworn to any falsehood, however injurious and diabolical, without mental reservation. Iachimo's confession in the last scene is too wordy and tediously prolonged, and the humility of it is scarcely in accordance with his character, as portrayed in the earlier scenes of the play

These three characters are the principal ones of that group to which the attention is chiefly attracted, Cymbeline, himself, is represented as weak and vacillating— a mere tool of his wicked queen, who says 'I never do him wrong, but he does buy my injuries,' rewards her for them, as if they were benefits : this woman is utterly villainous without any redeeming quality, unless affection for her foolish and unprincipled son be called one, it is seldom that Shakespeare draws such characters, for he loves rather to elevate than to depress humanity, and to paint in sunbeams, than to people twilight with forms of darkness Perhaps she is introduced to bring the sweet character of the pure and loving Imogen into greater prominence by the power of contrast The conduct of Cymbeline is unaccountable, save in a timid and wavering mind; having beaten the Romans by accident, he is amazed at his own temerity, and, in the very triumph of victory, makes a peace, and promises to pay to Cæsar the tribute which he had gone to war to avoid.

Cloten has been said to be so singular a character,
and possessed of qualities so contradictory, that he
has been supposed to form an exception to Shakespeare's usual integrity in copying from nature.   We
cannot see in what particular he is irreconcilable to humanity , he is a knave, a braggart, and a fool in most
matters, but that is no reason why he should not possess some shrewd common sense ideas occasionally
Nothing can be happier than his defiance of the Roman
ambassador —'If Cæsar can hide the sun from us
with a blanket, or put the moon in his pocket, we will
pay him tribute for light , else, sir, no more tribute '
Quaintly expressed, certainly, but unanswerable as an
argument, it is not Cloten's want of sense, but his
outrageous vanity, that makes him ridiculous   He is
not half so great a contradiction to himself as is Polonius in 'Hamlet,' and yet we can easily understand
the peculiarities of that character , the weakness of
age consuming the strength of maturity, folly encroaching on wisdom , in Cloten, it is folly consuming common sense   Shakespeare requires no justification to
the observing mind , few men are either all wisdom or
all folly , the writings of the wisest man of whom we
have any record are bitter condemnations of his own
actions, eloquent laments for time misspent in voluptuous abandonment   We doubt not that the poet drew
Cloten from a living model , singularities, in works of
fiction, are generally copied from life—they are flights
too bold for most authors to take without precedent
Respecting the character of Cloten, Hazlitt has remarked 'that folly is as often owing to a want of proper
sentiments as to a want of understanding '
  In the delineation of the two princes, Guiderius and
Arviragus, Shakespeare propagates a doctrine which

will find many opponents in the present day · he infers
that there is an innate loyalty of nature, a sovereignty
in blood in those born of a kingly stock , and the young
princes brought up as simple rustics, and born of a
weak uxorious father, are represented as feeling their
high birth so strongly that it impels them to acts of
heroism.   Belarius says :

> 'Their thoughts do hit
> The roofs of palaces; and nature prompts them,
> In simple and low things, to prince it much
> Beyond the trick of others.'

Their old protector is a courtier, turned hermit from
an acute sense of wrong and a consequent disgust of
civilized life, and his language is that of one who has
seen the world to satiety   he is full of bitter reflections
on princes and their courts, where oft a man gains ill
report for doing well, and 'must court'sey at the censure '   He bears some resemblance to the moralizing
Jaques , all natural objects suggest to him lofty and
religious reflections, and the low-roofed cave which
makes him bow as he issues from it to greet the rising
sun, instructs him to adore its great Creator.   Jaques
had been a libertine in his youth, and Belarius is
guilty of a dishonorable and wicked revenge by bring-
ing up the sons of Cymbeline as rustics ; the father
had injured him, but he had robbed the children of
their birthright.

PAINE, PINX.

IRA ALDRIDGE AS AARON.

Titus Andronicus, Act IV, Scene II.

HISTORICAL SUMMARY OF 'TITUS AN-DRONICUS.'

THIS sanguinary and disgusting tragedy is still suf-fered to retain its place among the works of Shake-speare, although it is rejected by all the commentators and critics except Capell and Schlegel. The editors of the first folio edition, however, have included it in that volume, which implies that they considered the play as his production. George Meres enumerates it among his works in 1598, and this author was person-ally esteemed and consulted by our poet. It is now generally supposed that the present drama found ad-mission into the original complete edition of Shake-speare's works only because he had written a few lines in it, assisted in its revisal, or produced it on the stage. A tradition to this effect is mentioned by Ravenscroft in the preface to his alteration of this tragedy, as acted at Drury Lane in 1687, where he says, ' I have been told by some anciently conversant with the stage, that it was not originally Shakespeare's, but was brought by a private author to be acted , and he gave only some master-touches to one or two of the principal parts ' The events of this drama are not of historical occurrence, but were probably borrowed from an old ballad on the same subject entered on the books of the Stationers' Company in 1593, about which period it appears to have been written Mr.

Malone has marked with double inverted commas
those passages in which he supposes the hand of
Shakespeare may be traced

It is recorded of the poet Robert Burns that, 'when
in his fifteenth year, Mr. Murdoch, his school-teacher,
sometimes visited the family at Mount Oliphant, and
brought books with him. On one occasion he read
'Titus Andronicus' aloud, but Robert's pure taste rose
in a passionate revolt and protest against its coarse
cruelties and repugnant horrors '

Alexander Smith's 'Life of Burns '

PERSONS REPRESENTED

SATURNINUS, son to the late emperor of Rome, and
    afterwards declared emperor himself
BASSIANUS, brother to Saturninus, in love with La-
    vinia.
TITUS ANDRONICUS, a noble Roman, general against
    the Goths.
MARCUS ANDRONICUS, tribune of the people and
    brother to Titus.
LUCIUS,
QUINTUS,
MARTIUS,   } sons to Titus Andronicus.
MUTIUS,
YOUNG LUCIUS, a boy, son to Lucius.
PUBLIUS, son to Marcus the tribune.
ÆMILIUS, a noble Roman
ALARBUS,
CHIRON,   } sons to Tamora.
DEMETRIUS,

AARON, a Moor, beloved by Tamora
CAPTAIN, TRIBUNE, MESSENGER, and CLOWN; Romans
Goths and Romans

TAMORA, queen of the Goths
LAVINIA, daughter to Titus Andronicus
NURSE, and a black Child.

Kinsmen of Titus, Senators, Tribunes, Officers, Soldiers, and Attendants

SCENE, Rome, and the country near it

COMPENDIUM OF THE PLAY.

TITUS ANDRONICUS, a Roman general, in a successful campaign against the Goths, takes captive their queen Tamora with her three sons, and conveys them to Rome in triumph, where one of the youths is inhumanly sacrificed by the conqueror at the tomb of his children who had been slain in battle Eager for revenge, the artful Tamora makes a favorable impression on the heart of the emperor Saturninus, and becomes the partner of his throne By the contrivance of her two sons and a Moorish paramour named Aaron, she procures the assassination of Bassianus, the emperor's brother, while his wife Lavinia, the daughter of Titus, is deprived of her tongue and hands by the Gothic princess, in order to prevent a discovery of the ill usage which she had previously sustained Two

sons of Titus shortly after suffer death for their supposed participation in the murder of Bassianus the
real perpetrators are at length discovered , and the
enraged father, having decoyed the young men to his
house, puts a period to their existence, and serves up
their mangled relics to their mother in a banquet.
The unfortunate Lavinia falls by the hand of her
father, who afterwards sacrifices the empress to his
fury, for which he is slain by Saturninus, who in his
turn loses his crown and life by the sword of Lucius,
the only surviving son of Titus, who procures a repeal
of his banishment by means of a Gothic army, and is
proclaimed emperor by the senate and people

We forbear comment on this tragedy

MARIANA.

Pericles, Prince of Tyre. Act IV, Scene I.

HISTORICAL SUMMARY OF 'PERICLES'

THE History of Apollonius, king of Tyre, contained in an old book of the fifteenth century entitled *Gesta Romanorum*, appears to have formed the ground-work of the present drama Gower, in his *Confessio Amantis*, has related the same story, the incidents and antiquated expressions of which may here be distinctly traced , and hence, as Gower himself is introduced to perform the office of Chorus, it seems reasonable to conjecture that the work of the old poet has been chiefly followed

That the greater part of this production was the composition of Shakespeare is rendered highly prob-able by the elaborate disquisitions of Steevens and Malone, who have decided, from the internal evidence, that he either improved some older imperfect work, or wrote in connection with some other author ; that it contains more of his language than any of his doubted dramas , that many scenes throughout the whole piece are his, and especially the greater part of the last three acts ; and that what he did compose was his earliest dramatic effort, being assigned to the year 1590 The external evidences are, that Edward Blount, one of the printers of the first folio Shakespeare, entered ' Pericles' at Stationers' Hall in 1608, though it appeared the next year from another publisher, with Shakespeare's name in the title-page , that it was acted at Shakespeare's own theatre, the Globe , and that it is ascribed to him by several authors near his time This play is not to be found in the folio of 1623, the editors having probably forgotten it until the book was printed, as they did 'Troilus and Cressida,' which is inserted in the volume, but not in the Table of Contents

The text of this play is so wretchedly corrupt, that it does not so much seem to want illustration as emendation, in which little assistance can be obtained from the inspection of the earliest printed copies, which appear in so imperfect a form that there is scarcely a single page undisfigured by the grossest errors

'On the whole,' says Mr Steevens, 'were the intrinsic merits of 'Pericles' yet less than they are, it would be entitled to respect among the curious in dramatic literature As the engravings of Mark Antonio are valuable, not only on account of their beauty, but because they are supposed to have been executed under the eye of Rafaelle , so 'Pericles' will continue to owe some part of its reputation to the touches it is said to have received from the hand of Shakespeare.'

PERSONS REPRESENTED

ANTIOCHUS, king of Antioch.
PERICLES, prince of Tyre
HELICANUS, } two lords of Tyre.
ESCANES,
SIMONIDES, king of Pentapolis
CLEON, governor of Tharsus.

LYSIMACHUS, governor of Mitylene.
CERIMON, lord of Ephesus
THALIARD, lord of Antioch
PHILEMON, servant to Cerimon
LEONINE, servant to Dionyza.
MARSHAL
A PANDER, and his WIFE
BOULT, their servant
GOWER, as Chorus

DAUGHTER OF ANTIOCHUS
DIONYZA, wife to Cleon.
THAISA, daughter to Simonides.
MARINA, daughter to Pericles and Thaisa
LYCHORIDA, nurse to Marina
DIANA

Lords, Ladies, Knights, Gentlemen, Sailors, Pirates,
Fishermen, and Messengers, etc

SCENE, dispersedly in various countries.

COMPENDIUM OF THE PLAY

ANTIOCHUS, king of Antioch, in order to keep his
daughter unmarried, subjects all suitors to the penalty
of death who fail to expound a riddle which is recited
to each · the beauty and accomplishments of the young
princess overcome all their apprehensions, and prove
fatal to many   At length, Pericles, prince of Tyre,
explains the riddle to the monarch, who determines to
reward his ingenuity by procuring his assassination.

To avoid the impending danger, which he is unable to resist, and to preserve his territories from invasion, Pericles quits his kingdom, and arrives at Tharsus, where his timely interposition preserves Cleon and his subjects from the horrors of famine He is afterwards driven by a storm on the shore of Pentapolis, where he marries Thaisa, the daughter of king Simonides, who, in accompanying her husband to his kingdom, is delivered of a daughter at sea, named Marina. The body of Thaisa, who is supposed to be dead, is enclosed in a box by her disconsolate husband, and committed to the waves, which drive it towards the coast of Ephesus, where Cerimon, a compassionate and skilful nobleman, succeeds in restoring the vital functions of the lady, who afterwards becomes the priestess of Diana In the meantime, Pericles commits his infant to the custody of Cleon and his wife, and embarks for Tyre. At the age of fourteen, Marina excites the jealousy of her guardians by the superiority of her attainments, which obscures the talents of their own daughter a ruffian is accordingly hired to deprive her of life, who is about to execute his orders, when she is rescued from destruction by pirates, who hurry her to Mitylene; at which place she is recognized by her father, who, deceived by the representations of his perfidious friends, is bitterly lamenting her supposed death By the directions of the goddess Diana, who appears to him in a dream, he repairs to Ephesus, where he recovers his long-lost Thaisa, and unites his daughter in marriage to Lysimachus, the governor of Mitylene, while Cleon and his wife fall victims to the fury of the enraged populace.

EDWIN FORREST AS KING LEAR.

King Lear, Act IV., Scene II.

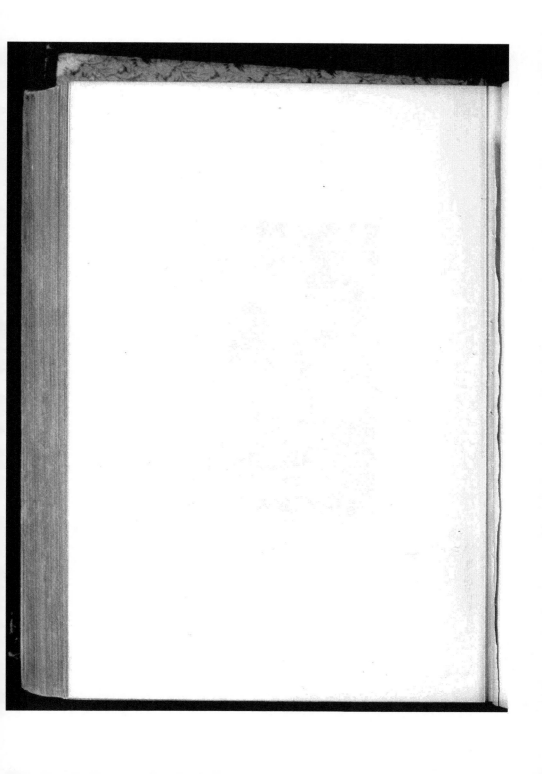

A.HECKEL, PINX.

CORDELIA AND KING LEAR.

King Lear. Act I, Scene I.

FROM A PHOTOGRAPH BY B. SARONY.

MISS WAINWRIGHT AS JULIET.

Romeo and Juliet. Act II. Scene II.

HISTORICAL SUMMARY OF 'ROMEO AND JULIET.'

THE story on which this play is founded is related as a true one in Girolamo de la Corte's 'History of Verona' In 1562 Mr. Arthur Brooke published a poem on 'the Tragicall Historic of Romeus and Juliett;' the materials for which he chiefly obtained from a French translation, by Boisteau, of an Italian novel by Luigi da Porto, a gentleman of Vicenza, who died in 1529. A prose translation of Boisteau's work was also published in 1567, by Painter, in his 'Palace of Pleasure;' and on the incidents of these two works Shakespeare is supposed to have constructed this interesting tragedy. Malone imagines that the present piece was designed in 1591, and finished in 1596; but Chalmers refers it to 1592, and Dr. Drake to 1593. There are four early editions of it in quarto, namely those of 1597, 1599, 1609, and one without date; the first of which is less copious than the others, since each successive edition appears to have been revised, with additions to particular passages

PERSONS REPRESENTED.

ESCALUS, prince of Verona.
PARIS, a young nobleman, kinsman to the prince.
MONTAGUE, } heads of two houses, at variance with
CAPULET, }   each other.

OLD MAN, uncle to Capulet

ROMEO, son to Montague

MERCUTIO, kinsman to the prince, and a friend to Romeo.

BENVOLIO, nephew to Montague, and a friend to Romeo

TYBALT, nephew to Lady Capulet

FRIAR LAURENCE, a Franciscan

FRIAR JOHN, of the same order

BALTHASAR, servant to Romeo

SAMPSON,
GREGORY, } servants to Capulet

ABRAM, servant to Montague.

APOTHECARY

THREE MUSICIANS

CHORUS BOY , PAGE to Paris ; PETER , an OFFICER

LADY MONTAGUE, wife to Montague

LADY CAPULET, wife to Capulet

JULIET, daughter to Capulet.

NURSE to Juliet

Citizens of Verona , several Men and Women, relations to both houses , Maskers, Guards, Watchmen, and Attendants

SCENE, during the greater part of the play, in Verona , once in the fifth act, at Mantua

COMPENDIUM OF THE PLAY.

THE violent feuds subsisting at Verona between the powerful families of the Capulets and Montagues form

no obstruction to the establishment of a mutual attachment between Romeo, the only son of Montague, and
Juliet, the heiress of the house of Capulet. A secret
marriage appears to realize their fond anticipations of
felicity, when Tybalt, a nephew of Capulet, rouses the
indignation of the young bridegroom by the murder
of his friend Mercutio, and falls a sacrifice to his
resentment in single combat This outrage subjects
Romeo to a sentence of banishment by the prince,
while the unsuspecting relatives of Juliet, attributing
her grief to the loss of her cousin, resolve to divert
her melancholy by an immediate marriage with Count
Paris Finding her parents inexorable to every
entreaty of delay, the unfortunate lady repairs to the
cell of Friar Laurence, who had married her; and
receives from his hands a powerful soporific, causing a
temporary suspension of the vital functions for two
and forty hours. On the day appointed for the
nuptials, Juliet is discovered stiff and cold, and is conveyed, amidst the tears of her family, to the cemetery
of her ancestors The good friar, in the meantime,
despatches a messenger to the residence of Romeo at
Mantua, arranging his secret return to his native city
before the expiration of Juliet's sleep But the
destiny of the lovers is misfortune ; the letter of Friar
Laurence never reaches its destination ; and the distracted husband, learning from another source the
death of his mistress, hastens to Verona, forces an
entrance in the obscurity of night to the monument of
the Capulets, takes poison, and expires, soon after
which the friar arrives to await the recovery of Juliet
from her trance, who, reviving to a sense of her hope-
less woe, and seeing the dead body of Romeo stretched
before her, finds means to terminate her existence by

plunging the dagger of her husband into her heart. The rival families now too late bewail their miserable infatuation and, at the intercession of the prince, bury their animosities in a treaty of peace and alliance

No one can fail to admire the admirable construction of this tragedy of our poet, had it been merely a love story, it would have run the risk of becoming tedious, how artfully this is obviated! The broils of the rival factions of Capulet and Montague, extending even to their humblest retainers, the high spirits of Mercutio, with his lively wit and florid imagination, the unconquerable pugnaciousness of Tybalt, 'the very butcher of a silk button,' the garrulous coarseness of the Nurse, and the peevishness of old Capulet, all these give a briskness and rapidity to the early scenes of the play, while the latter ones are, as they should be, almost confined to the afflictions of the two lovers.

Romeo is an idealization of the early youth of genius, he is, in truth, a poet in his love We fancy that Shakespeare wrote it with a vivid recollection of some early attachment of his own, and that Romeo utters the intense and extravagant passion which a gifted, but affectionate nature, such as Shakespeare might have given way to, before the judgment of maturer years had calmed down this frantic tyranny of love

The poet has been censured for making Juliet Romeo's second love, and Garrick, in his adaptation of the play, cut out all allusion to Rosaline, whom Romeo first loves, with as much earnestness, and even more extravagance than that which he displays in his subsequent passion for Juliet But his love for Rosaline was a mere creation of fancy, the feverish

FROM A PHOTOGRAPH BY GILBERT & BACON.

MAURICE BARRYMORE AS ROMEO.

Romeo and Juliet, Act II., Scene II.

excitement of a nature, to which love was a necessity, in her he worshipped an ideal of his own warm imagination, which painted her as an angel amongst women. Shakespeare also indulges a gentle satire on the too positive convictions of youth. Romeo declares his unalterable fidelity to Rosaline, and trusts that when his eyes admit that they have seen her equal, his tears will turn to fire, and burn the 'transparent heretics,' and yet, in one brief hour from this time, even at the first glance, he transfers his love to Juliet But we can easily forgive this fickleness, we feel angry at the haughty Rosaline, who 'hath forsworn to love,' for her cold rejection of the passionate affection of Romeo, and pleased that he has found one who receives and returns his passion His poetic and fervent affection deserves the love which the generous Juliet bestows upon him, and how tender, how devoted, how utterly unselfish is her passion, how modestly beautiful and delicate is her apology for the immediate confession of it.

> Thou know'st the mask of night is on my face,
> Else would a maiden blush bepaint my cheek,
> For that which thou hast heard me speak to-night.
> Fain would I dwell on form; fain, fain deny
> What I have spoke. But farewell compliment!

There is no affected coyness, no frigid conventionality in her demeanor, she is a child of nature yielding to the sweet impulses of a first love, and proclaiming her passion to the object of it with the unrestrained sincerity of an innocent and confiding spirit Her impatience for the arrival of her husband on the evening of their nuptials has been censured as inconsistent with a becoming modesty, and not to be

reconciled with the natural timidity of a young maiden,
even of Juliet's warm and impetuous nature Mr.
Hazlitt has finely answered this objection, he says—
'Such critics do not perceive that the feelings of the
heart sanctify, without disguising, the impulses of
nature Without refinement themselves, they con-
found modesty with hypocrisy.' How admirably also
does Shakespeare provide for every improbable circumstance, and not only takes away their improbability,
but renders them highly consistent and natural, thus
when Juliet drinks the potion which is to consign her,
a living woman, to a loathsome tomb, she is made to
work upon her own imagination by a vivid picture of
the horrors of her incarceration in the vault where the
festering remains of all her 'buried ancestors are
packed' and at length swallows the potion in a
paroxysm of terror

The naturalness of the incident is also heightened
by the first introduction of the Friar gathering medicinal herbs, and descanting upon their nature and
properties It is likely that he who was so well acquainted with the uses of 'baleful weeds and precious
juic'd flowers' would employ them to carry out a
difficult and dangerous stratagem Shakespeare seldom
omits an opportunity for the utterance of any instructive truth or moral maxim, he was the educator
of his audiences, and it gives us a higher opinion of
the playgoers of his time to know that they were
pleased with the introduction of severe moral truths
into their amusements The language of this Friar is
full of them, how fine is the reflection which crosses
his mind when going forth in the early dawn to gather
his medicinal herbs, and how naturally it arises out of
the situation ·

O. VERMEHREN, PINX.

ROMEO AND JULIET.

Act III., Scene V.

For nought so vile that on the earth doth live,
But to the earth some special good doth give,
Nor aught so good, but, strained from that fair use,
Revolts from true birth, stumbling on abuse.

Mercutio is one of Shakespeare's peculiarities, one
of the favorite children of his sportive fancy, bred in
the sunshine of his finely balanced mind   The mer-
curial and brilliant nature of the Veronese gentleman
is full of that natural gladness, that 'overflow of
youthful life, wafted on over the laughing waves of
pleasure and prosperity,' which few authors besides
Shakespeare impart to their creations   Well might
Dr. Johnson say that his comedy seems to be instinct

It may certainly be wished that the language given
to Mercutio was less coarse and sensual than it frequently is, but this licentiousness of conversation is
consistent with the probable humor of a man in the
summer of life, in perfect health, and devoid of all
anxiety, and, however repugnant to modern ideas of
delicacy and gentlemanly breeding, is perhaps a picture
of the discourse of the young nobles and gallants of
Shakespeare's own time

An instance of our poet's power of strongly deline-
ating a character in a few lines, is to be seen in his
introduction of the poor apothecary, who is as original a
conception, and during his brief scene, wins upon the
sympathy of the audience, as much as the hero of the
story himself

This, like most of our poet's tragedies, preaches a
stern moral, it shows like a beacon-fire, to warn the
young from unsanctioned love and idolatrous passion.
Shakespeare probably intended to punish the lovers
for the deception they both practised upon indulgent

parents, while the parents are, through their children, scourged for their vain feuds and unreasonable hatred The young die after the first brief hour of joy, the old live on, childless and desolate, to repent the blind malignity which has wrecked the happiness of them all.

H.MERLE,PINX.

HAMLET AND OPHELIA.

Hamlet. Act III., Scene I.

HISTORICAL SUMMARY OF 'HAMLET'

THE French novelist Belleforest extracted from Saxo Grammaticus, the Danish historian, the history of 'Amleth,' and inserted it in the collection of novels published by him in the latter part of the sixteenth century, whence it was translated into English under the title of 'The Historie of Hamblett,' a small quarto volume printed in black letter, which formed the subject of a play previous to 1589, and on these materials our author is supposed to have constructed this noble tragedy, the composition of which is assigned by Malone to the date of 1600, while Mr Chalmers and Dr Drake contend that it was written as early as 1597, on the authority of Dr. Percy's copy of Speght's edition of 'Chaucer,' which once belonged to Gabriel Harvey, who had written his name at both the commencement and conclusion, with several notes between; among which was the following The younger sort take much delight in Shakespeare's 'Venus and Adonis,' but his 'Lucrece,' and his tragedy of 'Hamlet, Prince of Denmarke,' have it in them to please the wiser sort, 1598. The original composition of this play may, therefore, be placed in 1597, and its revision, with additions, in 1600. The earliest entry of it at Stationers' Hall is July 26, 1602; and a copy of the play in its imperfect state, dated 1603, and supposed to have been printed from a spurious original, was first

discovered in the beginning of 1825   Another edition
appeared in 1604, 'newly imprinted, and enlarged to
almost as much again as it was,' the variations in
which are both numerous and striking

PERSONS REPRESENTED.

CLAUDIUS, king of Denmark.
HAMLET, son to the former, and nephew to the present
    king
POLONIUS, lord chamberlain
HORATIO, friend to Hamlet
LAERTES, son to Polonius
VOLTIMAND,
CORNELIUS,
ROSENCRANTZ, } courtiers.
GUILDENSTERN,
OSRIC, a courtier.
ANOTHER COURTIER
A PRIEST
MARCELLUS, }
BERNARDO, } officers.
FRANCISCO, a soldier
REYNALDO, servant to Polonius
CAPTAIN   AMBASSADOR
GHOST of HAMLET'S FATHER.
FORTINBRAS, prince of Norway

GERTRUDE, queen of Denmark, and mother of Hamlet.
OPHELIA, daughter of Polonius

Lords, Ladies, Officers, Soldiers, Players, Grave-diggers, Sailors, Messengers, and other Attendants.

SCENE, Elsinore

COMPENDIUM OF THE PLAY.

THE sudden death of Hamlet king of Denmark, and the hurried and indecent nuptials of his widow with his brother and successor, fill the mind of the young prince Hamlet with grief and shame, which is speedily exchanged into a desire of revenge because of the appearance of his father's spirit, which informs the astonished youth that his end has been effected by the operation of poison, administered to him in his sleep by his perfidious brother. Doubtful of the truth of this supernatural communication, Hamlet counterfeits madness in order to conceal his designs, and invites the king and his court to witness the performance of a play which bears a striking similarity to the murder detailed by the Ghost Struck by the reproaches of a wounded conscience, the guilty monarch betrays the emotions of his mind to the vigilance of Hamlet, who is prevented from the prosecution of his revenge by the death of Polonius, the father of Ophelia, who is commissioned by the king to lie in ambush during an interview between the prince and his mother: Hamlet, hearing a noise, and conjecturing that it proceeds from his concealed uncle behind the arras, stabs the old man to the heart; a mistake, which deprives Ophelia of reason, and causes her self-

28

destruction ; while the unfortunate prince is banished to England by the king, who sends thither secret orders for his death on his arrival The accomplishment of this cruel mandate is prevented by his captivity by pirates, who land him on the Danish coast. In the meantime, Laertes, the son of Polonius, in his anxiety to revenge the deaths of his father and sister, tarnishes the natural generosity of his character by listening to the insidious suggestions of the king, who accomplishes the destruction of his nephew by means of a poisoned weapon, with which he is wounded in a trial of skill in fencing with Laertes, to which the unsuspecting youth is invited , and in which his antagonist also becomes the victim of his own fraud. Finding his end fast approaching, Hamlet inflicts on his uncle the just punishment of his atrocities , and soon after expires, after witnessing the untimely death of his mother by poison

Mr. Steevens estimates the character of Hamlet very sternly, and considers him not only unamiable but criminal , though he admits that the prince assassinated Polonius by accident, yet he states that he deliberately procures the execution of his two schoolfellows, who appear to have been ignorant of the treacherous nature of the mandate they were employed to carry , his conduct to Ophelia deprives her both of her reason and her life, and he then interrupts her funeral. and insults her brother by boasting of an affection for his sister which he had denied to her face, and that he kills the king at last to revenge himself, and not his father.

This summary of the character of Hamlet, though strongly stated, is not a false one , his conduct is certainly indefensible unless we regard him as a man

FROM A PHOTOGRAPH BY SMALL.

CHARLES FECHTER AS HAMLET.

Hamlet, Act V, Scene I.

whose mind was to some extent overthrown by the
peculiarity of the circumstances in which he was
placed This brings us to the oft disputed question,
whether the madness of Hamlet was real or feigned—
an attentive perusal of the tragedy will, we think, lead
us to the conclusion that it was both one and the
other His mind at times trembled on the brink of
madness, shaken but not overthrown Not utterly
perverted by mental disease, but very far from the
exercise of its healthy functions, at times enjoying the
perfect use of reason, and at others clouded and confused Hamlet exaggerates his mental defects, and
feeling his mind disordered, plays the downright madman   .

He, however, nowhere admits his insanity , and his
soliloquies certainly bear no appearance of wildness
So far from believing himself mad, he has great faith
in his own intellectual resources he feels that he is
surrounded by spies—by men whom he will trust as he
will ‘adders fanged ,’ but, he adds—

> It shall go hard,
> But I will delve one yard below their mines,
> And blow them at the moon

This implies great confidence in his own acuteness ,
and, to his mother, he most emphatically denies that
he labors under mental disorder he is, he says, ‘not
in madness, but mad in craft ’ But we should not
take the word of a madman for evidence respecting his
own malady Hamlet is rather cunning than wise—a
quality not unfrequently found in men suffering from a
partial mental alienation It should be recollected,
also, that he has no reason for assuming insanity to his
friend Horatio, whom he had trusted with his secret,

and informed that he might think fit 'to put an antic
disposition on' Still, when discoursing very gravely
with him in the church-yard, he suddenly breaks off
from his subject, and asks, abruptly—'Is not parch-
ment made of sheep-skins?' A mind so flighty cannot be justly called sound

Dr. Johnson says, 'of the feigned madness of
Hamlet there appears no adequate cause, for he does
nothing which he might not have done with the
reputation of sanity He plays the madman most
when he treats Ophelia with so much rudeness, which
seems to be useless and wanton cruelty.' This is true
enough, Hamlet's assumed madness in no way assists
in working out his revenge, but, on the contrary,
nearly prevents its execution, for had the king succeeded in his design in sending him to England, the
pretended lunacy would have brought him to his
death, or it might very likely have led to his close
confinement in Denmark. This absence, then, of a
sufficient cause for feigning madness implies that
some seeds of absolute insanity were the origin of it.

Hamlet's conduct to Polonius is very unjustifiable,
only to be accounted for by supposing that his mind is
somewhat disturbed, though he may also dislike the
old courtier because he is the counsellor and companion
of the king; but there is no treachery in the talkative
old man. Polonius is very just and open, when he
discovers Hamlet's love for his daughter, he lays no
plot to induce him to marry her, he will not play 'the
desk or table-book,' but discountenances the attachment, and informs the king and queen of it Foolishly
talkative, he is still a very shrewd man, and though
his wisdom is fast falling into the weakness and child-
ishness of age, he has been a very acute observer.

J. WAGREZ, PINX.

OPHELIA.

Hamlet, Act IV. Scene V.

Dr Johnson, who has given an admirable delineation
of this character, says : ' Such a man is positive and
confident, because he knows that his mind was once
strong, and he knows not that it has become weak
Such a man excels in general principles, but fails in the
particular application He is knowing in retrospect,
and ignorant in foresight. While he depends upon his
memory, and can draw from his repositories of knowledge, he utters weighty sentences and gives useful
counsel , but as the mind, in its enfeebled state, cannot
be kept long busy and intent, the old man is subject to
sudden dereliction of his faculties, he loses the order
of his ideas, and entangles himself in his own thoughts,
till he recovers the leading principle and falls again
into his former train. This idea of dotage encroaching
upon wisdom will solve all the phenomena of the
character of Polonius '

Ophelia is a gentle, affectionate character, drawn in
and sucked down by the whirlpool of tragic events
which surround her   Hamlet treats her very harshly,
but, although this probably proceeds partly from his
aberration of intellect, he is also influenced by a
suspicion that she is acting treacherously towards him,
and is an instrument in the hands of the king and her
father for some unworthy purpose

It has puzzled many of the critics to account for the
circumstance, that although Ophelia is so modest in
her sanity that she never even confesses her love for
Hamlet, we only gather from her actions that she
loves him ; that when she becomes insane she sings
snatches of obscene songs   Some have thought
Shakespeare erred in this, but in the expression of
human passions he never errs   It has been well suggested, that in madness people frequently manifest a

disposition the very opposite of that which they possessed while in a state of sanity—the timid become bold, the tender cruel—and that Ophelia, in like manner, forsook her modesty of demeanor, and became the reverse of her natural character Mr G. Dawson thinks Ophelia, in her sanity, to be warm in her passions—not a coarse sensualist, like the queen, but what he calls *sensuous*—that way disposed, yet keeping a strict guard upon herself, and that when she becomes mad that restraint is removed, and her character appears in its natural colors

Much controversy also has been expended upon the question whether the queen was an accessory to the murder of her husband, her surprise on Hamlet's exclamation in her chamber, 'As kill a king,' has been quoted to exonerate her. This supposition is strengthened by the fact, that she exhibits no uneasiness or remorse at the play, as the king does, and that no remark ever takes place between her and her husband in relation to it Her agony of mind when her son compares her two husbands, and so severely censures her, arises from the recollection of her adulterous intercourse with Claudius during the life of the late king, and her hasty and incestuous marriage

HUGO KONIG. PINX.

DESDEMONA'S DEFENCE.

Othello, the Moor of Venice. Act I. Scene III.

HISTORICAL SUMMARY OF 'OTHELLO'

A STORY in Cynthio's novels is the prototype whence our author derived his materials for this sublime and instructive tragedy, which is assigned by Malone, after considerable hesitation, to the date of 1604, while Dr. Drake and Mr. Chalmers conjecture it to be the production of a period as late as 1612 or 1614. This play was first entered at Stationers' Hall Oct. 6, 1621, and appeared in quarto in the course of the following year, between which edition and the folio of 1623 many minute differences exist

'The beauties of this play,' says Dr Johnson, 'impress themselves so strongly on the attention of the reader, that they can draw no aid from critical illustration   The fiery openness of Othello, magnanimous, artless, and credulous, boundless in his confidence, ardent in his affection, inflexible in his resolution, and obdurate in his revenge, the cool malignity of Iago, silent in his resentment, subtle in his designs, and studious at once of his interest and his vengeance, the soft simplicity of Desdemona, confident of merit and conscious of innocence, her artless perseverance in her suit, and her slowness to suspect that she can be suspected, are such proofs of Shakespeare's skill in human nature, as, I suppose, it is vain to seek in any modern writer.   The gradual progress which Iago makes in the Moor's conviction, and the circumstances which he employs to inflame him, are so artfully natural, that, though it will perhaps not be said of him as he says of himself, that he is 'a man not easily jealous,' yet we cannot but pity him, when at last we find him 'perplex'd in the extreme '

PERSONS REPRESENTED.

DUKE OF VENICE
BRABANTIO, a senator
TWO OTHER SENATORS
GRATIANO, brother to Brabantio
LODOVICO, kinsman to Brabantio.
OTHELLO, the Moor.
CASSIO, his lieutenant
IAGO, his ancient
RODERIGO, a Venetian gentleman.
MONTANO, Othello's predecessor in the government
    of Cyprus
CLOWN, servant to Othello
HERALD

DESDEMONA, daughter to Brabantio, and wife to
    Othello
EMILIA, wife to Iago
BIANCA, a courtesan, mistress to Cassio

Officers, Gentlemen, Messengers, Musicians, Sailors,
    Attendants, etc

SCENE, for the first act, in Venice, during the rest
    of the play, at a seaport in Cyprus.

FROM A PHOTOGRAPH BY WALKER.

MRS. F. BERNARD-BEERE. AS DESDEMONA.

Othello the Moor of Venice. Act III. Scene IV.

COMPENDIUM OF THE PLAY

A MOORISH general in the service of the Venetians, named Othello, by his valor and mental accomplishments, captivates the affections of Desdemona, the only daughter of an eminent senator, who exposes herself to the resentment of an incensed father by eloping with her lover and becoming his wife These nuptials are no sooner solemnized than Othello is required by the senate to assume the command of Cyprus, whither he is followed by Desdemona, whose influence over her husband is exerted in behalf of Cassio, who has been deprived of his lieutenancy for an act of indiscretion, into which he has been betrayed by the devices of Iago, in order that he may at once gratify his diabolical malignity and promote his personal advancement by instilling groundless suspicions into the ear of his commander of a criminal attachment subsisting between his wife and Cassio, which he substantiates by so much seeming honesty of purpose and the production of such strong external testimony, that the fierce desire of revenge in the bosom of the Moor stifles the generous sympathies of his nature, and he smothers his innocent wife, leaving the assassination of Cassio to be effected by the agency of his supposed friend, who however fails to accomplish his deadly purpose The villany of Iago is at length brought to light by his wife Emilia, who is stabbed by her enraged husband, while the unfortunate Othello finds means to elude the vigilance of his attendants, and deprive himself of life by a concealed dagger In the meantime, Cassio is advanced to the government of Cyprus, and Iago is sentenced to expiate his crimes by a painful and protracted death

The Moor is amiable, brave, generous, and firm, with him, what should be, must be he will not permit his feelings to interfere with what he deems his duty This feature of his character contributes materially to the catastrophe of the tragedy had he possessed the irresolution of Hamlet, Iago's villany would have been discovered and Desdemona saved, for Hamlet would always have been desiring more evidence, and even, when convinced of her falseness, would have remained undecided how to act, and probably would have ultimately divorced her But Iago calculates on the hot Moorish blood which runs in Othello's veins, he knows the impetuous fierce passions which he latent in the soul of the victim of his fiendish deception, and practises upon them accordingly Othello is very philosophical until his mind is poisoned by the insinuations of Iago, he keeps a sort of military guard over his passions, remember his calm even conduct when Brabantio approaches him in the street at night, followed by armed servants and public officers, whom he bids to seize the Moor, he himself addressing him as 'vile thief,' and with other violent language And before the duke he conducts his own cause with the subtilty and readiness of an advocate. What a touch of effective oratorical artifice is that where he tells the assembled senate that he had been bred in a camp, knew but little of the world, and therefore could not grace his cause by the arts of eloquence; thus leading them to the belief that he was incapable of defending himself, and then delivering the most effective oration that could have been uttered in his behalf.

FROM A PHOTOGRAPH BY N. SARONY.

EDWIN BOOTH AS IAGO.

Othello, the Moor of Venice, Act I. Scene III.

But when the maddening conviction of his wife's treachery and shame is forced upon him, he breaks out into a paroxysm of frantic passion, his habit of self-government is for a time annihilated, and the hot blood of the savage triumphs over the judgment of the man   He tries to escape from this dreadful conviction :

'By heaven, I would most gladly have forgot it '

But Iago draws the web gradually closer and more closely around him, and, with fiendish sagacity, keeps the subject in all its most hideous colors perpetually in his mind until the final perpetration of the terrible catastrophe of the drama   How painfully affecting is the anguish of soul with which he exclaims : 'But yet the pity of it, Iago !—O, Iago, the pity of it, Iago !'   Well might Coleridge, with the true feeling of a poet, ask, as the curtain drops, which do we pity most, Desdemona, or the heart-broken Moor ?

Iago is an utter villain, with no redeeming circumstances—love, benevolence, sympathy for his race, every holy and exalted feeling have, in him, no existence, their place is occupied by a satanic selfishness and an absolute love of malice, it is the fertile activity of his intellect, and the ingenuity of his wickedness, that alone make him endurable, otherwise we should shrink from him with loathing and disgust.   He is the most villanous character ever drawn by Shakespeare, for Richard III. is cruel, to serve his ambition, but Iago is cruel and fraudulent, because he finds a pleasure in fraud and cruelty ; he has no belief in honesty—does not think there is any such thing in the world, he entertains an obdurate incredulity as to the virtue of women, and has a per-

fect faith that Desdemona will be seduced by Cassio,
if he tempts her   He looks upon everything only in
a gross and sensual light, and delights in painting the
purest feelings in the most repulsive colors   This will
explain why Shakespeare has put so many coarse and
revolting speeches in his mouth.   No character the
great poet ever drew utters so many offensive expressions, and this was, doubtless, intended to exhibit the
intense depravity of his mind   He has a natural turn
for dishonesty and trickery, and would rather gain his
ends by deception than by straightforward conduct.
He is proud of his cunning, and witty also, full of that
ill-natured sarcasm which delights in giving pain to
others

The character of Cassio is admirably delineated—he
is every way calculated to become an object of suspicion to the Moor—he is young, handsome and courte-
ous, a scholar, and something of a poet, as his beautiful description of Desdemona will evidence   Even
Iago admits, 'That he hath all those requisites in
him that folly and green minds look after '

Poor Desdemona is the perfection of womanly gentleness and tenderness—a generous, romantic girl, full
of kindness to every one, and by the very liberality
of her nature, laying herself open to the aroused suspicions of her husband   If she has a fault, it is that
she is too passive   Observe the wide contrast between
her character and that of Emilia, as finely portrayed
in the third scene of the fourth act.   Othello has de-
sired his wife to retire and dismiss her attendant and
the two women are conversing before they separate for
the night   Desdemona, in her simple purity, asks .

'Dost thou in conscience think,—tell me, Emilia,—
That there be women do abuse their husbands
In such gross kind.'

Note the worldliness of the other's reply ; she would
not do 'such a thing for a joint-ring,' *but*, etc , and
Desdemona's sceptical rejoinder, 'I do not think there
is any such woman.' The absolute purity of her mind
will not permit her to believe in evil How sweetly
touching is her character compared with that of Iago—
a seraph and a demon.

INDEX TO THE CHARACTERS

IN

SHAKESPEARE'S DRAMATIC WORKS.

————◆◆————

Aaron,	A Moor, beloved by Tamora,	Titus Andronicus.
Abbot of Westminster,		Richard II.
Abergavenny, Lord,		King Henry VIII.
Abhorson,	An Executioner,	Measure for Measure.
Abram,	Servant of Montague,	Romeo and Juliet
Achilles,	A Grecian Commander,	Troilus and Cressida.
Adam,	Servant to Oliver,	As You Like it.
Adrian,	A Lord of Naples,	Tempest
Adriana,	Wife of Antipholus of Ephesus,	Comedy of Errors.
Ægeon,	A Merchant of Syracuse,	Comedy of Errors
Æmilia,	An Abbess at Ephesus,	Comedy of Errors.
Æmilius,	A Noble Roman,	Titus Andronicus
Æmilius Lepidus	A Roman Triumvir,	Julius Cæsar
Æneas,	A Trojan Commander,	Troilus and Cressida.
Agamemnon,	A Grecian General,	Troilus and Cressida.
Agrippa,	A Friend of Cæsar,	Antony and Cleopatra.
Agrippa Menenius,	Friend of Coriolanus,	Coriolanus
Ague cheek, Sir Andrew		Twelfth Night.
Ajax,	A Grecian Commander,	Troilus and Cressida.
Alarbus,	Son of Tamora,	Titus Andronicus
Albany, Duke of		King Lear.
Alcibiades,	An Athenian General,	Timon of Athens
Alencon, Duke of,		King Henry VI , Part I.
Alexander,	Servant to Cressida,	Troilus and Cressida
Alexander Iden,	A Kentish Gentleman,	King Henry VI , Part II.
Alexas,	Attendant on Cleopatra,	Antony and Cleopatra.
Alice,	Attendant on Prin. Katharine,	King Henry V.
Alonso,	King of Naples,	Tempest
Amiens,	Attendant on Exiled Duke,	As You Like it
Andromache,	Wife of Hector,	Troilus and Cressida.
Andronicus, Marcus,	Tribune, Brother of Titus,	Titus Andronicus.
Andronicus, Titus	General against the Goths,	Titus Andronicus
Angelo,	A Goldsmith,	Comedy of Errors
Angelo,	Deputy of Duke of Vienna,	Measure for Measure.
Angus,	A Scottish Nobleman.	Macbeth
Anne, Lady,	Widow of Edward Prin of Wales,	King Richard III
Anne Bullen,	Afterwards Queen,	King Henry VIII
Antenor	A Trojan Commander,	Troilus and Cressida.
Antigonus,	A Sicilian Lord	Winter's Tale.
Antiochus,	King of Antioch,	Pericles.
Antiochus,	Daughter of	Pericles.

220

Benvolio,	Friend of Romeo,	Romeo and Juliet
Berkley, Earl.		King Richard II.
Bernardo,	An Officer,	Hamlet.
Bertram,	Count of Rousillon,	A'l's Well that Ends Well.
Bianca,	Mistress of Cassio,	Othello
Bianca,	Sister of Katherine,	Taming of the Shrew.
Bigot, Robert,	Earl of Norfolk,	King John
Biondello,	Servant of Lucentio,	Taming of the Shrew.
Biron,	Attendant on King of Navarre,	Love's Labour Lost.
Bishop of Carlisle,		King Richard II.
Bishop of Ely,		King Henry V.
Bishop of Ely,	John Morton,	King Richard III
Bishop of Lincoln,		King Henry VIII.
Bishop of Winchester,	Gardiner,	King Henry VIII.
Blanch,	Niece of King John,	King John
Blount, Sir James,		King Richard III.
Blunt, Sir Walter,	Friend of Henry IV,	Henry IV, Parts I, II.
Bolingbroke,	A Conjurer,	King Henry VI, Part II.
Bolingbroke,	Afterwards Henry IV	King Richard II
Bona,	Sister of the French Queen,	Henry VI, Part III.
Borachio,	Follower of Don John,	Much Ado About Nothing
Bottom,	The Weaver,	Midsummer Nights Dream
Boult,	A Servant,	Pericles.
Bourbon, Duke of,		King Henry V
Bouchier, Cardinal,	Archbishop of Canterbury,	King Richard III
Boyet,	Attendant on Princess of France,	Love's Labour Lost.
Brabantio,	A Senator,	Othello
Brakenbury, Sir Robt,	Lieutenant of the Tower,	King Richard III.
Brandon		King Henry VIII.
Brutus, Junius,	Tribune of the People,	Coriolanus
Brutus, Marcus,	A Roman Conspirator,	Julius Cæsar
Buckingham, Duke of,		King Richard III
Buckingham, Duke of,	Of the King's Party,	King Henry VI, Part II
Buckingham, Duke of,		King Henry VIII
Bullcalf,	A Recruit,	King Henry IV, Part II.
Bullen, Anne,	Afterwards Queen,	King Henry VIII
Burgundy, Duke of,		King Henry V
Burgundy, Duke of,		King Henry VI, Part I
Burgundy, Duke of,		King Lear
Busby,	"Creature" of Richard II,	King Richard II
Butts, Dr,	Physician to Henry VIII,	King Henry VIII.
Cade, Jack,	A Rebel,	King Henry VI., Part II.
Cadwal	Arviragus in Disguise,	Cymbeline
Cæsar, Octavius,	A Triumvir,	Antony and Cleopatra.
Caithness,	A Scottish Nobleman,	Macbeth.
Caius, Dr,	A French Physician,	Merry Wives of Windsor
Caius, Lucius,	General of Roman Forces,	Cymbeline
Caius M Coriolanus,	A Noble Roman,	Coriolanus
Calchas,	A Trojan Priest,	Troilus and Cressida.
Caliban,	A Savage and Deformed Slave,	The Tempest
Calphurnia,	Wife of Cæsar,	Julius Cæsar
Cambridge, Earl of,	A Conspirator,	King Henry V.
Camillo,	A Sicilian Lord,	Winter's Tale
Campeius, Cardinal,		King Henry VIII
Camidius,	Lieutenant General of Antony,	Antony and Cleopatra.
Canterbury, Archb of,	Cardinal Bouchier,	King Richard III
Canterbury, Archb of,		King Henry V
Canterbury Archb. of,	Cranmer,	King Henry VIII.

Count of Ronsillon,	. . . . .	All's Well that Ends Well.
Countess of Auvergne,	.	King Henry VI , Part I.
Countess of Rousillon,	Mother of Bertram,	All's Well that Ends Well.
Court,	Soldier in King's Army,	King Henry V
Cranmer, . .	. Archbishop of Canterbury,	King Henry VIII
Cressida, . .	Daughter to Chalcas,	. Troilus and Cressida.
Cromwell, . .	. Servant to Wolsey, . .	. King Henry VIII
Curan, .	A Courtier, .	King Lear
Curio, .	. Attendant on Duke of Illyria,	Twelfth Night
Curtis, .	. Servant to Petruchio, .	. Taming of the Shrew.
Cymbeline, .	King of Britain, . .	. Cymbeline
Dame Quickly, .	Hostess of a Tavern,	. King Henry IV , Pts I&II.
Dardanius, .	. Servant to Brutus,	. Julius Cæsar
Dauphin, The, .	Louis, .	. King John
Davy, . .	. Servant to Shallow,	. King Henry IV , Part II.
Decius Brutus,	A Roman Conspirator,	. Julius Cæsar
Deiphobus, .	Son to Priam,	. Troilus and Cressida
Demetrius, .	Friend to Antony,	. Antony and Cleopatra.
Demetrius, .	In Love with Hermione,	Midsummer Nights Dream
Demetrius, .	Son to Tamora,	. Titus Andronicus.
Dennis, .	Servant to Oliver, .	. As You Like it
Denny, Sir Anthony,	. . .	. King Henry VIII
Dercetas, .	Friend to Antony, . .	Antony and Cleopatra.
Desdemona, .	. Wife to Othello,	. Othello
Diana, . .	. Daughter to Widow,	All's Well that Ends Well.
Diana, . .	. .	. Pericles
Dick, . .	. A Follower of Jack Cade,	. King Henry VI , Part II.
Diomedes, .	. A Grecian Commander,	. Troilus and Cressida.
Diomedes, .	Attendant on Cleopatra,	Antony and Cleopatra.
Dion, . .	. A Sicilian Lord,	. Winter's Tale
Dionyza, . .	. Wife to Cleon,	. Pericles
Doctor Butts, .	. Physician to Henry VIII ,	King Henry VIII
Doctor Caius, .	A French Physician,	. Merry Wives of Windsor.
Dogberry, .	. A Foolish Officer, .	. Much Ado About Nothing.
Doll Tearsheet,	A Bawd, . .	. King Henry IV , Part II.
Dolabella, .	Friend to Cæsar, .	Antony and Cleopatra
Domitius Enobarbus,	Friend to Antony,	. Antony and Cleopatra.
Don Adriano de Armado,	A Fantastical Spaniard,	Love's Labour Lost
Don John, .	Bastard Brother to Don Pedro,	Much Ado About Nothing.
Don Pedro, .	. Prince of Aragon,	Much Ado About Nothing.
Donaldbain, .	Son to King Duncan, .	. Macbeth.
Dorcas, .	A Shepherdess,	. Winter's Tale
Dorset, Marquis of,	. . .	King Richard III
Douglas, Earl of	Archibald, .	King Henry IV , Part I.
Dromio of Ephesus	⎱ Twin Brothers Attendants on	⎱ Comedy of Errors
Dromio of Syracuse,	⎰ the two Antipholuses,	⎰
Duchess of Gloster,	. . .	King Richard II.
Duchess of York,	.	King Richard II
Duchess of York,	Mother to King Edward IV., .	King Richard III.
Duke, The, .	. Living in Exile,	As You Like it
Duke of Albany,	.	King Lear
Duke of Alencon,	.	. King Henry VI , Part I.
Duke of Aumerle,	. Son to Duke of York,	. King Richard II
Duke of Bedford,	Brother to King Henry V ,	. King Henry V
Duke of Bedford,	Regent of France, .	King Henry VI , Part I.
Duke of Bourbon,	. . . .	King Henry V
Duke of Buckingham,	.	. King Richard III
Duke of Buckingham,	Of the King's Party, .	. King Henry VI , Part I.

Earl of Warwick,	Of the York Faction,	Henry VI , Pts I , II , III.
Earl of Westmoreland,	Friend to King Henry IV ,	Henry IV , Parts I , II
Earl of Westmoreland,		King Henry V
Earl of Westmoreland,	Of the King's Party,	. Henry VI , Part III
Earl of Worcester,	. Thomas Percy,	. Henry IV , Parts I II.
Earl Rivers,		King Richard III
Edgar,	Son to Gloster,	. King Lear
Edmund,	. Earl of Rutland,	Henry VI , Part III
Edmund,	. Bastard Son to Gloster,	King Lear
Edmund Mortimer,	. Earl of March,	. King Henry IV , Part I
Edmund Mortimer,	Earl of March,	. King Henry VI , Part I.
Edmund of Langley,	. Duke of York,	. King Richard II
Edward,	. Prince of Wales,	. King Richard III
Edward,	. Son to Plantagenet,	. King Henry VI , Part II.
Edward Prince of Wales,	Son to King Henry VI ,	Henry VI , Part III
Edward IV , King,		. King Richard III
Edward Earl of March,	Afterwards King Edward IV ,	Henry VI., Part III.
Egeus,	Father to Hermia,	Midsummer Nights Dream
Eulamour,	. Agent for Silvia,	. Two Gentlemen of Verona.
Elbow,	A Simple Constable,	Measure for Measure
Eleanor,	. Duchess of Gloster,	King Henry VI , Part II.
Elinor,	. Mother to King John,	King John
Elizabeth,	. Queen to King Edward IV ,	King Richard III.
Ely, Bishop of,	. John Morton,	King Richard III
Ely, Bishop of,	.	King Henry V.
Emilia,	. Wife to Iago,	Othello
Emilia,	A Lady,	Winter's Tale
Enobarbus, Domitius,	Friend to Antony,	. Antony and Cleopatra.
Eros,	Friend to Antony,	Antony and Cleopatra
Erpingham, Sir Thomas,	Officer in the King's Army,	King Henry V
Escalus,	A Lord of Vienna,	Measure for Measure.
Escalus,	Prince of Verona,	. Romeo and Juliet.
Escanes,	A Lord of Tyre,	Pericles
Essex, Earl of,	. Geoffrey Fitz Peter,	King John
Euphronius,	An Ambassador,	Antony and Cleopatra.
Evans, Sir Hugh,	A Welsh Parson,	Merry Wives of Windsor.
Exeter, Duke of,	. Uncle to Henry V ,	King Henry V
Exeter, Duke of,	. Of the King's Party,	Henry VI , Part III.
Exiled Duke,	.	. As You Like it.
Fabian,	. Servant to Olivia,	Twelfth Night
Falstaff, Sir John,		Henry IV , Parts I , II.
Falstaff, Sir John,		Merry Wives of Windsor.
Fang,	A Sheriff's Officer,	King Henry IV , Part II.
Fastolfe, Sir John,		King Henry VI , Part I.
Falconbridge, Lady,	Mother to Robert and Philip,	King John.
Falconbridge, Philip,	Bastard Son to King Richard I ,	King John.
Falconbridge, Robert,	Son to Sir Robert Falconbridge,	King John
Feeble,	A Recruit,	King Henry IV , Part II.
Fenton,	. A Young Gentleman,	Merry Wives of Windsor.
Ferdinand,	. King of Navarre,	. Love's Labour Lost.
Ferdinand,	. Son to the King of Naples,	The Tempest.
Fitz-Peter, Geoffrey,	Earl of Essex,	. King John
Fitzwater, Lord,		King Richard II.
Flaminius,	. Servant to Timon,	Timon of Athens.
Flavius,	A Roman Tribune,	. Julius Cæsar
Flavius,	. Steward to Timon,	Timon of Athens.
Fleance,	. Son to Banquo,	. Macbeth
Florence, Duke of,		. All's Well that Ends Well.

Hamlet, . .	. Prince of Denmark,	Hamlet.
Harcourt, .	. Of the King's Party,	. King Henry IV , Part II.
Hastings, Lord,	Enemy to the King,	. King Henry IV , Part II
Hastings, Lord,	. Of the Duke's Party,	Henry VI , Part III
Hastings, Lord,		King Richard III
Hecate, . .	. A Witch, . . .	Macneth
Hector, . .	. Son to Priam, . .	Troilus and Cressida
Helen, . .	. Woman to Imogen, .	Cymbeline
Helen, . .	. Wife to Menelaus, .	Troilus and Cressida
Helena, . .	. A Gentlewoman, .	All's Well that Ends Well
Helena, . .	. In Love with Demetrius,	. Midsummer Nights Dream
Helenus, . .	. Son to Priam, . . .	Troilus and Cressida
Helicanus, .	. A Lord of Tyre, .	Pericles
Henry, .	. Earl of Richmond, .	. King Richard III
Henry Bolingbroke,	Afterwards King Henry IV ,	. King Richard II
Henry, Earl Richmond,	A Youth, . .	Henry VI , Part III.
Henry Percy,	Son to Earl of Northumberland,	King Richard II
Henry Percy (Hotspur),	Son to Earl of Northumberland,	Henry IV , Parts I , II
Henry Percy, .	. Earl of Northumberland,	. Henry IV , Parts I , II.
Henry, Prince,	. Son to King John, .	. King John
Henry, Prince of Wales,	Son to King Henry IV , .	. Henry IV , Parts I , II.
Henry IV , King,		Henry IV , Parts I , II.
Henry V , King,	. . . .	King Henry V
Henry VI , King,		Henry VI , Parts I , II
Henry VIII , King,	. . . .	King Henry VIII
Herbert, Sir Walter, .		King Richard III
Hermia, . .	. Daughter to Egeus,	Midsummer Nights Dream
Hermione, . .	Queen to Sicilia, .	. Winter's Tale
Hero, .	. Daughter to Leonato, .	. Much Ado About Nothing
Hippolyta, .	. Queen of the Amazons,	. Midsummer Nights Dream
Holofernes,	. A Schoolmaster, .	. Love's Labour Lost
Horatio, .	. Friend to Hamlet, .	. Hamlet.
Horner, Thomas,	. An Armourer, . .	King Henry VI , Part II
Hortensio, .	. Suitor to Bianca, .	. Taming of the Shrew
Hortensius, .	. A Servant, .	. Timon of Athens
Hostess, .	. Character in the Induction,	Taming of the Shrew
Hostess Quickly,	. Hostess of a Tavern, .	. Henry IV , Parts I , II .
Hotspur (Henry Percy),	Son to Earl of Northumberland,	Henry IV , Parts I , II
Hubert de Burgh,	. Chamberlain to King John,	King John
Hume, .	. A Priest, .	. King Henry VI , Part II
Humphrey, D of Gloster	Uncle to King Henry VI ,	. King Henry VI , Part II
Humphrey, Pr of Gloster	Son to King Henry IV ,	. King Henry IV , Part II.
Huntsmen, .	Characters in the Induction,	Taming of the Shrew
Iachimo, . .	. Friend to Philario, .	. Cymbeline.
Iago, .	Ancient to Othello, .	Othello
Iden, Alexander,	. A Kentish Gentleman,	. King Henry VI , Part II
Imogen, . .	Daughter to Cymbeline,	. Cymbeline
Iras, . . .	Attendant on Cleopatra,	Antony and Cleopatra.
Iris, . .	. A Spirit, .	The Tempest
Isabel	. Queen of France, .	King Henry V
Isabella, . .	. Sister to Claudio, .	. Measure for Measure
Jack Cade, . .	. A Rebel, .	King Henry IV , Part II.
James Gurney,	. Servant to Lady Falconbridge,	King John
Jamy, .	. Officer in King's Army,	King Henry V
Jaquenetta, .	. A Country Wench, .	. Love's Labour Lost
Jaques, . .	Son to Sir Roland de Bois,	. As You Like it
Jaques, . .	. An attendant on Exiled Duke,	As You Like it.

Morgan,	Belarius in disguise,	Cymbeline.
Morocco, Prince of,	Suitor to Portia,	Merchant of Venice.
Mortimer, Edmund,	Earl of March,	King Henry IV, Part I.
Mortimer, Edmund,	Earl of March,	King Henry VI, Part I.
Mortimer, Lady,	Daughter to Glendower,	King Henry IV., Part I.
Mortimer, Sir Hugh,	Uncle to Duke of York,	Henry VI, Part III
Mortimer, Sir John,	Uncle to Duke of York,	Henry VI, Part III.
Morton, John,	Bishop of Ely,	King Richard III
Morton,	Servant to Northumberland,	King Henry IV, Part II.
Moth,	A Fairy,	Midsummer Nights Dream
Moth,	Page to Armado,	Love's Labour Lost.
Mouldy,	A Recruit,	King Henry IV, Part II.
Mountjoy,	A French Herald,	King Henry V.
Mowbray, Thomas,	Duke of Norfolk,	King Richard II.
Mowbray, Lord,	Enemy to the King,	King Henry VI, Part II.
Mustardseed,	A Fairy,	Midsummer Nights Dream
Mutius,	Son to Titus,	Titus Andronicus.
Nathaniel, Sir,	A Curate,	Love's Labour Lost.
Nerissa,	Waiting-maid to Portia,	Merchant of Venice
Nestor,	A Grecian Commander,	Troilus and Cressida.
Norfolk, Duke of,		King Richard II. & III.
Norfolk, Duke of,	Of the Duke's Party,	Henry VI, Part III.
Norfolk, Duke of,		King Henry VIII
Northumberland, Lady,		King Henry IV, Part II.
Northumberland, Earl of,		King Richard II
Northumberland, Earl of, Enemy to the King,		King Henry IV., Part II.
Northumberland, Earl of, Henry Percy,		King Henry IV, Pts I. & II.
Northumberland, Earl of, Of the King's Party,		Henry VI., Part III.
Nurse of Juliet,		Romeo and Juliet.
Nym,	Soldier in King's Army,	King Henry V.
Nym,	A Follower of Falstaff,	Merry Wives of Windsor.
Oberon,	King of the Fairies,	Midsummer Nights Dream
Octavia,	Wife to Antony,	Antony and Cleopatra.
Octavius Cæsar,	A Roman Triumvir,	Julius Cæsar
Octavius Cæsar,	A Roman Triumvir,	Antony and Cleopatra.
Old Gobbo,	Father to Launcelot Gobbo,	Merchant of Venice.
Oliver,	Son to Sir Rowland de Bois,	As You Like it.
Olivia,	A Rich Countess,	Twelfth Night.
Ophelia,	Daughter to Polonius,	Hamlet.
Orlando,	Son to Sir Rowland de Bois,	As You Like it.
Orleans, Duke of,		King Henry V.
Orsino,	Duke of Illyria,	Twelfth Night.
Osric,	A Courtier,	Hamlet
Oswald,	Steward to Goneril,	King Lear.
Othello,	The Moor,	Othello
Overdone, Mrs	A Bawd,	Measure for Measure.
Owen Glendower,		King Henry IV, Part I.
Oxford, Duke of,	Of the King's Party,	Henry VI, Part III.
Oxford, Earl of,		King Richard III.
Page, Mr,	Gentleman dwelling at Windsor,	Merry Wives of Windsor.
Page, Mrs,		Merry Wives of Windsor
Page, Mrs Anne,	Daughter to Mrs. Page,	Merry Wives of Windsor.
Page, William,	Son to Mr Page,	Merry Wives of Windsor.
Pandarus,	Uncle to Cressida,	Troilus and Cressida
Pandulph, Cardinal,	The Pope's Legate,	King John.
Panthino,	Servant to Antonio,	Two Gentlemen of Verona.

Princess Katharine,	. Daughter to King Charles VI.,	King Henry V.
Princess of France,	. . . .	. Love's Labour Lost.
Proculeius, .	. Friend to Cæsar, . .	. Antony and Cleopatra.
Prophetess,	. Cassandra, .	. Troilus and Cressida.
Prospero, .	. Rightful Duke of Milan,	. The Tempest.
Proteus, .	. A Gentleman of Verona, .	. Two Gentlemen of Verona.
Publius, .	. A Roman Senator, .	. Julius Cæsar.
Publius, .	. Son to Marcus, . .	. Titus Andronicus.
Pucelle, Joan la,	. Joan of Arc, . .	. King Henry VI., Part I.
Puck, . .	. A Fairy, . . .	. MidsummerNightsDream
Pyramus, .	. A Character in the Interlude,	MidsummerNightsDream
Queen, . .	. Wife to Cymbeline, .	. Cymbeline.
Queen Elizabeth,	. Queen to King Edward IV.,	. King Richard III,
Queen Katharine,	. Wife to King Henry VIII.,	. King Henry VIII.
Queen Margaret,	. Wife to King Henry VI.,	Henry VI., Part III.
Queen of Richard II.,	. . .	. King Richard II.
Quickly, Mrs., .	. Hostess of a Tavern,	. Henry IV., Parts I., II.,
Quickly, Mrs.,	. A Hostess : Wife to Pistol,	. King Henry V.
Quickly, Mrs. .	. Servant to Dr. Caius, .	. Merry Wives of Windsor.
Quince, .	. The Carpenter, .	. MidsummerNightsDream
Quintus, .	. Son to Titus, .	. Titus Andronicus.
Rambures, . .	. A French Lord, .	. King Henry V.
Ratcliff, Sir Richard,	. . .	. King Richard III.
Regan, . .	. Daughter to King Lear, .	. King Lear.
Reignier, .	. Duke of Anjou, .	. King Henry VI., Part I.
Reynaldo, .	. Servant to Polonius,	. Hamlet.
Richard, .	. Son to Plantagenet,	. King Henry VI., Part II.
Richard, .	. Afterwards Duke of Gloster,	King Henry VI., Part III.
Richard, Duke of Gloster	Afterwards King Richard III.,	King Richard III.
Richard, Duke of York,	Son to King Edward IV.,	. King Richard III.
Richard Plantagenet,	Duke of York, . .	. Henry VI., Pts. I.,II.,III.
Richard II., King,	. . .	. King Richard II.
Richard III., King,	. . .	. King Richard III.
Richmond, Earl of,	. Afterwards King Henry VII.,	King Richard III.
Rivers, Earl,	. Brother to Lady Grey, .	. King Richard III.
Rivers, Lord,	. Brother to Lady Grey, .	. Henry VI., Part III.
Robert Bigot, .	. Earl of Norfolk, .	. King John.
Robert Falconbridge,	Son to Sir Robert Falconbridge,	King John.
Robin, .	. A Page to Sir John Falstaff,	. Merry Wives of Windsor.
Robin Goodfellow (Puck),	A Fairy, . .	. MidsummerNightsDream
Roderigo, .	. A Venetian Gentleman, .	. Othello.
Rogero, .	. A Sicilian Gentleman, .	Winter's Tale.
Romeo. .	. Son to Montague, .	. Romeo and Juliet.
Rosalind, .	. Daughter to the Banished Duke,	As You Like it.
Rosaline, .	. Attendant on Princess of France,	Love's Labour Lost.
Rosencrantz, .	. A Courtier, . .	. Hamlet.
Ross, Lord, .	. . .	. King Richard II.
Ross, .	. A Scottish Nobleman,	. Macbeth.
Rotheram, Thomas,	. Archbishop of York,	. King Richard III.
Rousillon, Count of,	. Bertram, .	. All's Well that Ends Well.
Rousillon, Countess of,	Mother to Bertram,	. All's Well that Ends Well.
Rugby, .	. Servant to Dr. Caius,	. Merry Wives of Windsor.
Rumour, .	. As a Prologue, .	. King Henry IV., Part II.
Salanio, . .	. Friend to Antonio and Bassanio.	Merchant of Venice.
Salarino, . .	. Friend to Antonio and Bassanio,	Merchant of Venice.
Salerio, . .	. A Messenger from Venice,	. Merchant of Venice.

Sir Thomas Lovell,	. . . . .	. King Henry VIII
Sir Thomas Vaughan,		. King Richard III
Sir Toby Belch, .	. Uncle to Olivia,	. Twelfth Night
Sir Walter Blunt,	. Friend to King Henry IV,	. Henry IV, Parts I, II.
Sir Walter Herbert, .		. King Richard III
Sir William Catesby, .	. . . .	. King Richard III
Sir William Glandsale,		King Henry VI, Part I.
Sir William Lucy,	. . .	. King Henry VI, Part I.
Sir William Stanley,	. . .	. Henry VI, Part III
Siward,	. Earl of Northumberland,	. Macbeth
Siward Young,	. Son to Siward	. Macbeth
Slender,	. Cousin to Justice Shallow,	. Merry Wives of Windsor
Smith the Weaver,	A Follower of Cade,	. King Henry VI, Part II
Snare, . .	. A Sheriff's Officer,	. King Henry IV, Part II
Snout, . .	. The Tinker, . .	. MidsummerNightsDream
Snug, . .	. The Joiner, . .	. MidsummerNightsDream
Solinus,	Duke of Ephesus,	. Comedy of Errors
Somerset Duke of,	Of the King's Party,	. Henry VI, Parts II, III.
Somerville, Sir John,	. . .	. Henry VI, Part III
Southwell, .	. A Priest,	. King Henry VI, Part II.
Speed, .	. A Clownish Servant,	. Two Gentlemen of Verona.
Stafford, Lord,	Of the Duke's Party,	. Henry VI, Part III
Stafford, Sir Humphrey,	. . .	King Henry VI Part II.
Stanley, Lord,	. . . .	. King Richard III
Stanley, Sir John,	. . . .	. King Henry VI, Part II.
Stanley, Sir William,	. . .	Henry VI, Part III
Starveling,	. The Tailor,	. MidsummerNightsDream
Stephano, .	A Drunken Butler .	The Tempest
Stephano, .	. Servant to Portia, .	. Merchant of Venice
Strato, .	. Servant to Brutus,	. Julius Cæsar
Suffolk, Duke of,	. Of the King's Party,	. King Henry VI, Part II.
Suffolk, Duke of,		King Henry VIII
Suffolk, Earl of,	. . . .	King Henry VI, Part I.
Surrey, Duke of,		. King Richard II
Surrey, Earl of, .	. Son to Duke of Norfolk,	King Richard III.
Surrey, Earl of, .		. King Henry VIII.
Sylvius,	. A Shepherd,	. As You Like it.
Talbot, John, .	. Son to Lord Talbot,	King Henry VI, Part I.
Talbot, Lord, .	. Afterwards Earl of Shrewsbury,	King Henry VI, Part I.
Tamora, . .	. Queen of the Goths,	. Titus Andronicus
Taurus, .	. Lieutenant General to Cæsar,	Antony and Cleopatra
Tearsheet, Doll, .	. A Band,	. King Henry IV, Part II.
Thaisa, .	. Daughter to Simonides,	Pericles
Thaliard, .	. A Lord of Antioch,	. Pericles.
Thersites, .	. A Deformed Grecian,	. Troilus and Cressida
Theseus, .	. Duke of Athens,	. Midsummer NightsDream
Thisbe, .	. A Character in the Interlude,	Midsummer NightsDream
Thomas,	A Friar	Measure for Measure
Thomas, D of Clarence,	Son to King Henry IV, .	King Henry IV, Part II
Thomas Horner,	. An Armourer, .	. King Henry VI, Part II
Three Witches, .	. . . .	. Macbeth
Thurio, .	. Rival to Valentine, .	Two Gentlemen of Verona.
Thyreus, .	. Friend to Cæsar, .	Antony and Cleopatra
Timandra, .	. Mistress to Alcibiades, .	. Timon of Athens.
Time, .	. As Chorus, .	. Winter's Tale
Timon, .	. A Noble Athenian, .	. Timon of Athens
Titania, .	. Queen of the Fairies, .	. MidsummerNightsDream
Titinius, .	. Friend to Brutus and Cassius,	Julius Cæsar.

Willoughby, Lord,	. . .	King Richard II
Winchester, Bishop of,	Gardiner, . .	. King Henry VIII
Wolsey, Cardinal,	. . .	. King Henry VIII
Woodville,	. Lieutenant of the Tower,	King Henry VI , Part I.
Worcester, Earl of,	. Thomas Percy, . .	Henry VI , Parts I , II
York, Archbishop of,	Scroop, . .	. Henry IV , Parts I , II.
York, Archbishop of,	Thomas Rotheram, .	. King Richard III.
York, Duchess of,		King Richard II
York, Duchess of,	Mother to King Edward IV ,	King Richard III.
York, Duke of,	. Cousin to the King,	King Henry V
York, Duke of,	Uncle to King Richard II ,	King Richard II
York, Duke of,	. Son to King Edward IV ,	King Richard III
Young Cato,	Friend to Brutus and Cassius,	Julius Cæsar
Young Clifford,	Son to Lord Clifford, .	. King Henry VI , Part II.
Young Marcius,	Son to Coriolanus, .	. Coriolanus.
Young Siward,	. Son to Siward, . .	. Macbeth.

p 185

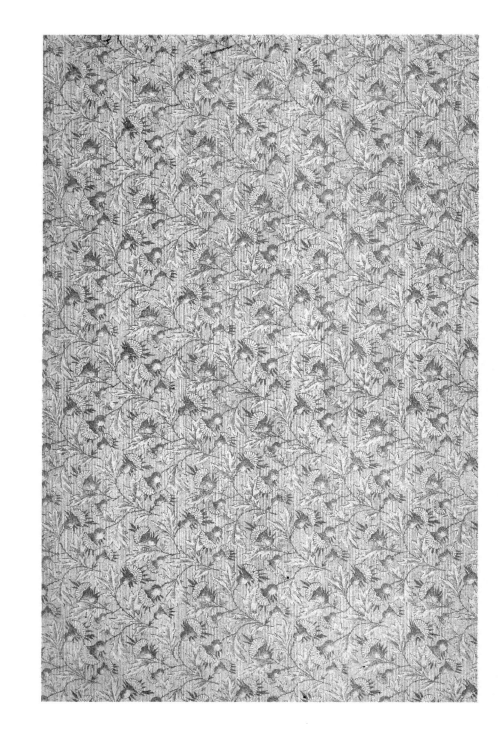

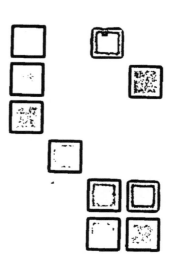

Lightning Source UK Ltd.
Milton Keynes UK
UKHW022032150822
407327UK00006B/1477